GLENCOE LANGUA

SPELLING POWER

GRADE 6

Glencoe McGraw-Hill

New York, New York   Columbus, Ohio   Woodland Hills, California   Peoria, Illinois

To the Student

This *Spelling Power* workbook provides the practice you need to improve your spelling and writing ability and to expand your vocabulary. Each spelling lesson focuses on a single spelling pattern or concept that applies to a list of words in a Word Bank. You then have several opportunities to practice what you've learned: writing the words, using them in sentences, recognizing and correcting them as you proofread, and applying the spelling pattern or concept to new words that follow the same pattern. If you have trouble with an exercise, you can always go back to the Word Bank and Key Concepts discussion, review the material, and then return to the exercise.

You can keep track of your own progress and achievement in spelling by using the Student Progress Chart, which appears on page v. With your teacher's help, you can score your work on any lesson, quiz, or test. After you know your score, use the Scoring Scale on pages vi–vii to figure your percentage. Then mark your score (or percentage correct) on the Student Progress Chart. Share your Progress Chart with your parents or guardians as your teacher directs.

Glencoe/McGraw-Hill

A Division of The **McGraw·Hill** *Companies*

Send all inquiries to:
Glencoe/McGraw-Hill
8787 Orion Place
Columbus, Ohio 43240

ISBN 0-07-826238-0

Printed in the United States of America

15 16   024   15 14 13 12 11 10 09

CONTENTS

STUDENT PROGRESS CHART

Fill in the chart below with your scores, using the scoring scale on the next page.

Name: _____

	Lesson	Pretest	Oral Quiz	Unit Review
1				
2				
3				
4				
Review				
5				
6				
7				
8				
Review				
9				
10				
11				
12				
Review				
13				
14				
15				
16				
Review				
17				
18				
19				
20				
Review				
21				
22				
23				
24				
Review				
25				
26				
27				
28				
Review				
29				
30				
31				
32				
Review				

SCORING SCALE

Use this scale to find your score. Line up the number of items with the number correct. For example, if 15 out of 16 items are correct, your score is 93.7 percent (see grayed area).

Number Correct

Number of Items	1	2	3	4	5	6	7	8	9	10	11	12	13	14	15	16	17	18	19	20
1	100																			
2	50	100																		
3	33.3	66.7	100																	
4	25	50	75	100																
5	20	40	60	80	100															
6	16.7	33.3	50	66.7	83.3	100														
7	14.3	28.6	42.9	57.1	71.4	85.7	100													
8	12.5	25	37.5	50	62.5	75	87.5	100												
9	11.1	22.2	33.3	44.4	55.6	66.7	77.8	88.9	100											
10	10	20	30	40	50	60	70	80	90	100										
11	9.1	18.1	27.2	36.3	45.4	54.5	63.6	72.7	81.8	90.9	100									
12	8.3	16.7	25	33.3	41.7	50	58.3	66.7	75	83.3	91.7	100								
13	7.7	15.3	23.1	30.8	38.5	46.1	53.8	61.5	69.2	76.9	84.6	92.3	100							
14	7.1	14.3	21.4	28.6	35.7	42.8	50	57.1	64.3	71.4	78.5	85.7	92.8	100						
15	6.7	13.3	20	26.7	33.3	40	46.6	53.3	60	66.7	73.3	80	86.7	93.3	100					
16	6.3	12.5	18.8	25	31.2	37.5	43.7	50	56.2	62.5	68.7	75	81.2	87.5	93.7	100				
17	5.9	11.8	17.6	23.5	29.4	35.3	41.2	47	52.9	58.8	64.7	70.6	76.5	82.3	88.2	94.1	100			
18	5.6	11.1	16.7	22.2	27.8	33.3	38.9	44.4	50	55.5	61.1	66.7	72.2	77.8	83.3	88.9	94.4	100		
19	5.3	10.5	15.8	21	26.3	31.6	36.8	42.1	47.4	52.6	57.9	63.1	68.4	73.7	78.9	84.2	89.4	94.7	100	
20	5	10	15	20	25	30	35	40	45	50	55	60	65	70	75	80	85	90	95	100
21	4.8	9.5	14.3	19	23.8	28.6	33.3	38.1	42.8	47.6	52.3	57.1	61.9	66.7	71.4	76.1	80.9	85.7	90.5	95.2
22	4.5	9.1	13.7	18.2	22.7	27.3	31.8	36.4	40.9	45.4	50	54.5	59.1	63.6	68.1	72.7	77.2	81.8	86.4	90.9
23	4.3	8.7	13	17.4	21.7	26.1	30.4	34.8	39.1	43.5	47.8	52.1	56.5	60.8	65.2	69.5	73.9	78.3	82.6	86.9
24	4.2	8.3	12.5	16.7	20.8	25	29.2	33.3	37.5	41.7	45.8	50	54.2	58.3	62.5	66.7	70.8	75	79.1	83.3
25	4	8	12	16	20	24	28	32	36	40	44	48	52	56	60	64	68	72	76	80
26	3.8	7.7	11.5	15.4	19.2	23.1	26.9	30.8	34.6	38.5	42.3	46.2	50	53.8	57.7	61.5	65.4	69.2	73.1	76.9
27	3.7	7.4	11.1	14.8	18.5	22.2	25.9	29.6	33.3	37	40.7	44.4	48.1	51.9	55.6	59.2	63	66.7	70.4	74.1
28	3.6	7.1	10.7	14.3	17.9	21.4	25	28.6	32.1	35.7	39.3	42.9	46.4	50	53.6	57.1	60.7	64.3	67.9	71.4
29	3.4	6.9	10.3	13.8	17.2	20.7	24.1	27.6	31	34.5	37.9	41.4	44.8	48.3	51.7	55.2	58.6	62.1	65.5	69
30	3.3	6.7	10	13.3	16.7	20	23.3	26.7	30	33.3	36.7	40	43.3	46.7	50	53.3	56.7	60	63.3	66.7
31	3.2	6.5	9.7	13	16.1	19.3	22.6	25.8	29	32.2	35.4	38.7	41.9	45.1	48.3	51.6	54.8	58	61.2	64.5
32	3.1	6.3	9.4	12.5	15.6	18.8	21.9	25	28.1	31.3	34.4	37.5	40.6	43.8	46.9	50	53.1	56.2	59.4	62.5
33	3	6	9	12.1	15.1	18.1	21.2	24.2	27.2	30.3	33	36.3	39.3	42.4	45.4	48.4	51.5	54.5	57.5	60.6
34	2.9	5.9	8.8	11.8	14.7	17.6	20.6	23.5	26.5	29.4	32.4	35.3	38.2	41.2	44.1	47.1	50	52.9	55.9	58.8
35	2.9	5.7	8.6	11.4	14.3	17.1	20	22.9	25.7	28.6	31.4	34.3	37.1	40	42.9	45.7	48.6	51.4	54.3	57.1
36	2.8	5.6	8.3	11.1	13.9	16.7	19.4	22.2	25	27.8	30.6	33.3	36.1	38.9	41.7	44.4	47.2	50	52.7	55.6
37	2.7	5.4	8.1	10.8	13.5	16.2	18.9	21.6	24.3	27	29.7	32.4	35.1	37.8	40.5	43.2	45.9	48.6	51.4	54
38	2.6	5.3	7.9	10.5	13.2	15.8	18.4	21.1	23.7	26.3	28.9	31.6	34.2	36.8	39.5	42.1	44.7	47.4	50	52.6
39	2.6	5.2	7.7	10.3	12.8	15.4	17.9	20.5	23.1	25.6	28.2	30.8	33.3	35.9	38.5	41	43.6	46.2	48.7	51.3
40	2.5	5	7.5	10	12.5	15	17.5	20	22.5	25	27.5	30	32.5	35	37.5	40	42.5	45	47.5	50

Number Correct

Number of Items

	21	22	23	24	25	26	27	28	29	30	31	32	33	34	35	36	37	38	39	40
1																				
2																				
3																				
4																				
5																				
6																				
7																				
8																				
9																				
10																				
11																				
12																				
13																				
14																				
15																				
16																				
17																				
18																				
19																				
20																				
21	100																			
22	95.4	100																		
23	91.3	95.6	100																	
24	87.5	91.6	95.8	100																
25	84	88	92	96	100															
26	80.8	84.6	88.5	92.3	96.2	100														
27	77.8	81.5	85.2	88.9	92.6	96.3	100													
28	75	78.6	82.1	85.7	89.3	92.9	96.4	100												
29	72.4	75.9	79.3	82.8	86.2	89.7	93.1	96.6	100											
30	70	73.3	76.7	80	83.3	86.7	90	93.3	96.7	100										
31	67.7	70.9	74.2	77.4	80.6	83.9	87.1	90.3	93.5	96.8	100									
32	65.6	68.8	71.9	75	78.1	81.2	84.4	87.5	90.6	93.8	96.9	100								
33	63.6	66.7	69.7	72.7	75.8	78.8	81.8	84.8	87.8	90.9	93.9	96.9	100							
34	61.8	64.7	67.6	70.6	73.5	76.5	79.4	82.4	85.3	88.2	91.2	94.1	97.1	100						
35	60	62.9	65.7	68.6	71.4	74.3	77.1	80	82.9	85.7	88.6	91.4	94.4	97.1	100					
36	58.3	61.1	63.8	66.7	69.4	72.2	75	77.8	80.6	83.3	86.1	88.9	91.7	94.4	97.2	100				
37	56.8	59.5	62.2	64.9	67.6	70.3	72.9	75.7	78.4	81.1	83.8	86.5	89.2	91.9	94.6	97.3	100			
38	55.3	57.9	60.5	63.2	65.8	68.4	71.1	73.7	76.3	78.9	81.6	84.2	86.8	89.5	92.1	94.7	97.3	100		
39	53.8	56.4	58.9	61.5	64.1	66.7	69.2	71.8	74.4	76.9	79.5	82.1	84.6	87.2	89.7	92.3	94.9	97.4	100	
40	52.5	55	57.5	60	62.5	65	67.5	70	72.5	75	77.5	80	82.5	85	87.5	90	92.5	95	97.5	100

Spelling Power

Lesson 1: Short Vowel Spellings

Word Bank

arid	benefit	static	text	complex
distract	vivid	unselfish	trusting	plot

Key Concepts

1. Short vowel sounds are often spelled with single vowel letters.

   <u>a</u>tt<u>i</u>c   bl<u>o</u>ck   <u>u</u>nr<u>e</u>st

2. Short vowel sounds include \a\ as in *hat*, \e\ as in *net*, \i\ as in *did*, \o\ as in *lot*, and \u\ as in *cup*.

Spelling Practice

Put the words from the Word Bank in alphabetical order. Then circle all short vowel sounds: \a\, \e\, \i\, \o\, and \u\.

1. _____
2. _____
3. _____
4. _____
5. _____

6. _____
7. _____
8. _____
9. _____
10. _____

Spelling in Context

Choose the word from the Word Bank that best completes each sentence. Write the word on the line.

1. Giving to charity is a(n) _____ deed.

2. Desert lands usually have a(n) _____ climate.

3. The _____ on our car radio was annoying.

4. Can I borrow your math _____ to finish my homework?

5. "I'm _____ you to keep your promise," said Dad.

LESSON 1 continued

Proofreading Practice

As you read the following paragraph, circle the five misspelled words. Write the correct spelling for each circled word on the lines.

My friend Nick and I were planning a plout for a mystery. I wanted to yell out my idea, but I was afraid I would destract him. The scene–quite vived in my mind–was very complix. I thought both of us might benifit if I drew a picture. "What a great idea!" Nick exclaimed when he looked at the drawing.

1. _____   3. _____   5. _____

2. _____   4. _____

Spelling Application

Below are eight more words that reflect the Key Concepts in the lesson. Find each hidden word in the word chain. Circle the words and then write them on the lines provided in the order in which they appear in the word chain. Circle the short vowels.

Example: sitentrust

sit   tent   trust

catnip   daffodil   encrust   knot
nonsense   pun   timid   trunk

catnipunonsensencrustrunknotimidaffodil

1. _____   5. _____

2. _____   6. _____

3. _____   7. _____

4. _____   8. _____

Spelling Power

Lesson 2: Long Vowel Spellings

Word Bank

deny	quote	theme	complaint	plead
oath	keen	migrate	twilight	thorough

Key Concepts
Long vowel sounds are often spelled with vowel combinations.

1. The \a\ sound may be spelled *ai or a__e*.
   rain   tape

2. The \e\ sound may be spelled *ea, ee, or e__e*.
   team   week   compete

3. The \i\ sound may be spelled *i, igh, i__e, or y*.
   bias   high   kite   why

4. The \o\ sound may be spelled *oa, ough, or o__e*.
   foam   though   nose

Spelling Practice

Put the words from the Word Bank in alphabetical order. Circle the letters that create the long vowel sounds.

1. _____   6. _____
2. _____   7. _____
3. _____   8. _____
4. _____   9. _____
5. _____   10. _____

Spelling in Context

Choose the word from the Word Bank that best completes each sentence. Write the word on the line.

1. Our family does a _____ cleaning job every spring.

2. I won't _____ the fact that I don't like housework.

3. "Dad and I don't want to hear one _____," said Mom.

4. As usual, my little brother began to _____ with me to help him clean his room.

5. By _____ everybody was tired and ready for a dinner out.

Name _____ Date _____ Class _____

Proofreading Practice

Read the paragraph below. Find the five misspelled words and circle them. Then, on the numbered lines, write the correct spelling for each circled word.

My sister Maria is kene on learning more about birds. She took an oeth to read one book about birds every week. The theem of one book was bird watching. The book explains why birds migreat to warm climates. To qouat Maria: "Sometimes I wish I could fly south for the winter too."

1. _____   3. _____   5. _____

2. _____   4. _____

Spelling Application

Listed below are ten more words that reflect the Key Concepts you have learned. Read each crossword puzzle clue. Then write the correct word from the word list in the puzzle squares.

bait   boast   Braille   dough   greed
lame   restyle   sighs   slide   teal

Across

1. special alphabet for the blind
4. breathes deeply
7. brag
8. unable to walk
10. food for fish
11. selfishness

Down

2. style again
3. mixture for baking
5. playground chute
6. dark blue green color

Spelling Power

Lesson 3: The Vowel *u*

Word Bank

unite	issue	juvenile	manual	cruise
document	gratitude	nuisance	routine	vacuum

Key Concept

The vowel *u* is used less frequently than *a, e, i,* or *o*. Try to visualize these words as you learn to spell them. Here's a trick to help you remember *vacuum*: It is the only common English word that has two *u*'s in a row.

Spelling Practice

Write the words from the Word Bank in alphabetical order.

1. _____   6. _____

2. _____   7. _____

3. _____   8. _____

4. _____   9. _____

5. _____   10. _____

Spelling in Context

Use context clues to determine which word from the Word Bank best completes each sentence. Write the word on the line.

1. The Declaration of Independence is a great historic _____.

2. An important campaign _____ is how to lower taxes.

3. In our city, a _____ cannot be out after 10:00 P.M. without an adult.

4. A pet owner can be fined if his or her dog becomes a _____ to neighbors.

5. My parents left for a _____ in the Caribbean.

LESSON 3 continued

Proofreading Practice

Read the letter. Find the five misspelled words and circle them. Then write the correct spelling for each circled word on the lines that follow.

Dear Mayor Gibson,

   We are writing to express our gratitood for your support of our school Science Fair. We are happy that you took time from your rootine activities to attend! Our favorite display showed how a vakume cleaner works. We thought watching the machine work was more interesting than reading the manool. All of us younite in thanking you!

Yours truly,

The students at Deergrove Middle School

1. _____ 3. _____ 5. _____

2. _____ 4. _____

Spelling Application

Below are six more words that reflect the Key Concept you have learned. Write the word whose meaning fits each set of terms.

| contribute | cruel | excuse | numerous | pursue | useful |

1. helpful, suitable, _____

2. chase, follow, _____

3. mean, unkind, _____

4. give, donate, _____

5. many, countless, _____

6. forgive, apologize, _____

Spelling Power

Lesson 4: Double Consonants

Word Bank

ballot	gossip	mammoth	accident	villain
occasion	essential	withheld	summarize	appropriate

Key Concepts

1. Double consonants often follow short vowel sounds.

   chu**bb**y   ye**ll**ow

2. Double consonants usually represent a single unit of sound.

   ski**pp**ing   fla**tt**en

3. Sometimes double consonants represent two units of sound.

   succeed (hard and soft *c*)

   fishhook (*sh* blend and *h*)

Spelling Practice

Put the words from the Word Bank in alphabetical order. Circle the double consonants in each word. Then write 2 or 3 to describe the Key Concept that applies to that word.

1. _____   2. _____

2. _____   4. _____

3. _____   6. _____

4. _____   8. _____

5. _____   10. _____

Spelling in Context

Choose the word from the Word Bank that best completes each sentence. Write the word on the line.

1. Every student gets a(n) _____ for the school election.

2. We were asked to _____ the story in our own words.

3. I don't like listening to _____ that might hurt others.

4. The police captured the _____ as he fled from the crime.

5. During a snowstorm, Mom drives slowly to avoid a(n) _____.

Name _____ Date _____ Class _____

LESSON 4 continued

Proofreading Practice

Read the ad that follows. Find and circle the five misspelled words. Then write the correctly spelled words on the lines below.

Come to Our Mammith Jacket Sale!

We have hundreds of jackets to sell. No stock is being witheld for next year! Our jackets are escential for any wardrobe. They are aproppriate for casual or formal events. Choose a jacket for your next special ockasion.

1. _____ 3. _____ 5. _____

2. _____ 4. _____

Spelling Application

Below are ten more words with double consonants. Find each word from the list and circle it in the puzzle. Then list the words on the lines. Write a 3 next to any words that are examples of Key Concept 3.

addition   allow   cabbage   classify   comment
knickknacks   pollute   sizzle   success   sudden

```
t k n i c k k n a c k s
n o l r e w o l l a t u
e e l z z i s a s b n c
m i g a t h s m a b e c
m k o i a s i r f a t e
o e d l i a d o t g u s
c d a f n s u d d e n s
a n y t a e t u l l o p
```

1. _____ 6. _____
2. _____ 7. _____
3. _____ 8. _____
4. _____ 9. _____
5. _____ 10. _____

8 Grade 6

Spelling Power

Copyright © by The McGraw-Hill Companies, Inc.

Name _____ Date _____ Class _____

Unit 1 Review
Lessons 1–4

arid	ballot	benefit	complaint	complex
deny	essential	issue	juvenile	mammoth
migrate	nuisance	routine	static	summarize
text	theme	thorough	unite	vivid

Choose the word from the word list above that best completes each sentence.

1. _____ lands have a shortage of rainfall.

2. Camels are _____ to people living in desert areas.

3. The camel's ability to carry heavy loads is a _____ to the desert dwellers.

4. A _____ camel owners have is that their animals often have bad tempers.

5. You can't _____ that those hard workers have a right to feel crabby sometimes.

6. During a camel's daily _____, stopping for food is not always possible.

7. Their _____ digestive system helps them go days without eating.

8. Providing food is not an _____ that camel owners have to deal with daily.

9. Desert sand can be a _____, but camels are lucky enough to have three eyelids.

10. To _____, camels are well-suited for desert life.

Use a word from the word list above to define the following phrases. Write the word on the line provided.

_____ **11.** main idea of a paper

_____ **12.** young person

_____ **13.** move or travel to another location

_____ **14.** join together

_____ **15.** instructive book

_____ **16.** omitting nothing

_____ **17.** strikingly bright

_____ **18.** election form

_____ **19.** huge

_____ **20.** scratchy electrical sound

Spelling Power

Proofreading Application

Lessons 1–4
As you read the story, find the twenty misspelled words and circle them. Then write the correct spelling for each circled word on the lines that follow.

Detective Shelly Sherlock was kean on solving mysteries. Today's problem was jewelry missing from Countess Lily's hotel room. First Shelly did a thorogh search for clues. She found an important documint in the countess's room. "The vilain might have left fingerprints on this," Shelly guessed.

Shelly worked until twylight completing her rutine search around the hotel. Quite by acident, she ran into a couple carrying some cleaning supplies. "What brings you here?" she asked.

"We're part of the cleaning crew for a special ocasion," they replied.

"Ah! the plat thickens!" thought Shelly. Trousting her intuition, she pretended that the couple was innocent. To destract them, she offered them some gum and then tossed the wrapper on the carpet. When they didn't pick it up, Shelly guessed they were not working for the hotel.

"I've heard some gosip about burglars. Have you seen anything strange?" As they looked at each other, Shelly knocked over their vacum cleaner. The contents spilled out. There were the countess's jewels!

"I pleed with you not to force us to talk!" the man begged. "We took an ooth to keep our boss's secret. It's not apropriate to talk about the boss."

"It's my duty to call the police," Shelly said. "I have never witheld evidence."

Later the countess showed her greatitude by inviting the detective to visit her in Paris. To quoet Shelly: "What an unselfush person!"

1. _____ 8. _____ 15. _____
2. _____ 9. _____ 16. _____
3. _____ 10. _____ 17. _____
4. _____ 11. _____ 18. _____
5. _____ 12. _____ 19. _____
6. _____ 13. _____ 20. _____
7. _____ 14. _____

Spelling Power

Lesson 5: The \s\ Sound with *c* or *s*

Word Bank

fantasy	consent	citizen	recent	vicinity
privacy	concise	incident	license	bicycle

Key Concept

The \s\ sound can be spelled with an *s* or with a *c* that is followed by an *e, i,* or *y.*

sa**ss**y	**s**ent	**s**i**s**ter	**s**orry
cent	spa**c**ious	fen**ce**	
city	re**c**ipe		
cy**c**le	fan**cy**		

Spelling Practice

Choose a word from the Word Bank to match each pronunciation. Write the word on the line.

Example: fan′ sē _____fancy_____

1. prī′ və sē _____
2. lī′ səns _____
3. kən sīs′ _____
4. bī′ sə kəl _____
5. vi sin′ ə tē _____

6. fan′ tə sē _____
7. in′ sə dənt _____
8. rē′ sənt _____
9. sit′ ə zən _____
10. kən sent′ _____

Spelling in Context

Choose the word from the Word Bank that best completes each sentence. Write the word on the line.

1. If your report is too wordy, you can make it more _____.

2. If you _____ to do something, you agree to do it.

3. If an event is _____, it did not happen long ago.

4. If your story is a _____, it can be called fiction.

5. If you enjoy being alone, you like your _____.

Name _____ Date _____ Class _____

Proofreading Practice

As you read the following news item, circle the five misspelled words. Write the correct spelling for each circled word on the lines below.

Youngster Helps Senior Sitizen

Mrs. Sylvia Yancy, who lives in the visinity of the police station, called to tell us about a recent insident in her neighborhood. Ricky Rice was riding his bisycle past her house just after getting his bike lisence at the station. As Ricky rode by, Mrs. Yancy tripped and was unable to get up. Ricky rode back to the station to ask for help. One police officer remarked, "He certainly is a sensible kid."

1. _____ 3. _____ 5. _____

2. _____ 4. _____

Spelling Application

Listed below are eight additional words that reflect the Key Concept in the lesson. Write each new word next to the word or phrase that defines it. Circle the letters that make the \s\ sound in each word.

centimeter	circulate	courtesy	cyclone
decide	senator	specify	spicy

1. peppery   _____

2. politeness   _____

3. describe in detail _____

4. distribute   _____

5. tornado   _____

6. legislator   _____

7. unit of measurement _____

8. make up mind   _____

Spelling Power

Lesson 6: The \k\ Sound with c, ck, ch, or qu

Word Bank

technique	chorus	frantic	architect	focus
character	dramatic	career	reckless	bouquet

Key Concept

The \k\ sound can be spelled with a c, ck, ch, or qu. Try to visualize these words as you learn to spell them.

critic   connect
wreck   package
chaos   anchor
boutique   croquet

Spelling Practice

Write the words from the Word Bank in alphabetical order. Circle the letters that represent the \k\ sound.

1. _____
2. _____
3. _____
4. _____
5. _____
6. _____
7. _____
8. _____
9. _____
10. _____

Spelling in Context

Choose the word from the Word Bank that best completes each sentence. Write the word on the line.

1. Our school's _____ sings for all holiday programs.

2. We are a little _____ when we haven't had enough time to rehearse.

Name _____ Date _____ Class _____

3. The director says, "Relax and _____ on the audience."

4. She is encouraging me to pursue a _____ in music.

5. To show our appreciation, we presented her with a _____ of roses.

Proofreading Practice

As you read the paragraph below, find and circle the five misspelled words. Then write the correct spelling for each circled word on the lines that follow.

I. M. Pei is a famous arckitekt. His building designs are meticulous drawings, not just recless sketches. He often uses a special technicue, combining shapes such as cubes and cylinders to achieve a dramatick effect. Mr. Pei used his design principles in creating the John F. Kennedy Library in order to to reflect the former president's strong caracter.

1. _____   **3.** _____   **5.** _____

2. _____   **4.** _____

Spelling Application

Listed below are six more words that contain the \k\ sound. Fill in the blanks with the word that best fits each meaning. After you have filled in the blanks, note that the letters in the squares form a word. Use that word to complete the sentence: "I am _____."

attic   chemist   clique   custard   educate   necklace

1. teach   _ _ ☐ _ _ _ _

2. pendant   ☐ _ _ _ _ _ _ _

3. top floor of some houses   _ _ _ ☐ _

4. close group of friends   _ _ _ ☐ _ _

5. pudding   _ ☐ _ _ _ _ _

6. one kind of scientist   _ _ ☐ _ _ _ _

Spelling Power

Spelling Power

Lesson 7: The \j\ Sound with *g* or *j*

Word Bank

genuine	justify	surgery	journal	energy
urge	legend	gigantic	majority	jealous

Key Concept

The \j\ sound can be spelled with a *j* or with a *g* that is followed by an *e, i,* or *y.*

jazz   jelly   jingle   jog   jump
gentle   gorgeous   garage
giant   tangible
gym   stingy

Spelling Practice

Write each word from the Word Bank under the letter that represents the \j\ sound.

j   ge   gi   gy

_____   _____   _____   _____

_____   _____

_____   _____

_____

Spelling in Context

Choose the word from the Word Bank that best completes each sentence. Write the word on the line.

1. The ten-story hospital is a _____ building.

2. Dad went there to have _____ on his knee.

3. While we waited, Mom read an interesting article in a medical _____.

4. She handed it to me and said, "I _____ you to read this."

5. I think my little sister was _____ of the attention I was getting.

LESSON 7 continued

Proofreading Practice

As you read the paragraph below, circle the five misspelled words. Then write the correct spelling for each of those words on the lines below.

Jackie Joyner-Kerse is a lejend in the history of women's sports. An Olympic gold-medal winner, she is a jenuine heroine in her hometown of East St. Louis. With boundless enerjy, she raised money to establish a club for boys and girls. The magority of visitors are amazed to see the fine gymnasium, library, and computer lab. Ms. Joyner-Kerse certainly did not need to gustify the expense of providing children with a fine place for learning and exercise.

1. _____ 3. _____ 5. _____

2. _____ 4. _____

Spelling Application

The eight words listed below contain the \j\ sound. Find each word in the word maze and draw a circle around the word. Then write the words on the lines.

genius   ginger   gymnast   heritage
janitor   job   junior   vegetable

```
m r e g d u j n r
v e g e t a b l e
a j a n i t o r g
h e r i t a g e n
b g t u l m r y i
i o t s a n m y g
r u j u n i o r s
```

1. _____ 3. _____

5. _____ 7. _____

2. _____ 4. _____

6. _____ 8. _____

Spelling Power

Lesson 8: Words with Silent Letters

Word Bank

knight	pledge	honorable	design	debt
autumn	heir	doubtful	folklore	knowledge

Key Concepts

1. Some words in the English language are difficult to spell because they contain silent, or unsounded, letters. The English spellings often reflect pronunciations from foreign languages.

   (Latin) *signum* → sign

   (Latin) *dubitare* → doubt

   (Latin) *columna* → column

   (Dutch) *knapzak* → knapsack

2. The letters *h*, *d*, and *l* are sometimes unsounded in English words.

   <u>h</u>onest   ri<u>d</u>ge   yo<u>l</u>k

Spelling Practice

Choose the word from the Word Bank that matches each pronunciation. Write the word on the line. Then circle the silent letter or letters in each word.

1. det _____
2. ār _____
3. nol'ij _____
4. fōk' lôr' _____
5. on' ər ə bəl _____
6. di zīn' _____
7. ô' təm _____
8. plej _____
9. nīt _____
10. dout' fəl _____

Spelling in Context

Choose the word from the Word Bank that best completes each sentence. Write the word on the line.

1. My favorite season of the year is _____.
2. It is _____ that a snowstorm will occur in September.

LESSON 8 continued

3. When you owe something, you have a _____ to repay.

4. Studying new subjects is a good way to gain _____.

5. What a beautiful _____ you drew!

Proofreading Practice

As you read the paragraph below, circle the misspelled words. Then write the correct spelling for those words on the lines below.

> Some of the foklore about King Arthur is based on real events. Every night in the king's court was expected to be onorable. They all took a plege to be loyal to their king. Together they sat at the Round Table to discuss problems and solutions. King Arthur hoped there would be an eir to the throne who would uphold his ideals.

1. _____   **3.** _____   **5.** _____

2. _____   **4.** _____

Spelling Application

Listed below are eight more words that contain unsounded letters. Use the words to complete the crossword puzzle that follows.

column	foreign	fudge	honest
knapsack	limb	plumber	yolk

Across
3. branch of a tree
4. storage bag carried on shoulders
7. candy made of milk, butter, and sugar
8. not native to a country

Down
1. the yellow part of an egg
2. truthful
5. worker who repairs water pipes
6. a newspaper feature

Spelling Power

Unit 2 Review
Lessons 5–8

architect	autumn	bicycle	bouquet	citizen
concise	doubtful	gigantic	heir	honorable
journal	justify	knight	legend	license
pledge	privacy	recent	reckless	surgery

For each sentence below, find the word from the list that best completes the sentence. Write the word in the blank.

1. Everybody in our class writes in a _____ daily.

2. To respect our _____, the teacher does not read our entries aloud.

3. We have learned to be _____ in our writing.

4. Last _____ Kevin wrote an article for the school newspaper.

5. The article was about a student who rode her _____ to school.

6. Gina Baker was hit by a _____ driver.

7. The doctors told Gina that she needed _____ on her leg.

8. It is _____ she'll be in the dance recital.

9. We sent her a get-well card and a _____ of roses.

10. Kevin thinks that the driver should lose his _____.

Look at the word list to find a synonym, or a word with a similar meaning, for each word that follows. Write the synonym in the blank.

11. inheritor   _____

12. myth   _____

13. huge   _____

14. trustworthy   _____

15. promise   _____

Use the remaining words from the word list to write five sentences of your own.

16. _____

17. _____

18. _____

19. _____

20. _____

Spelling Power

Proofreading Application

Lessons 5–8
As you read the following story, circle the twenty misspelled words. Write the correct spelling for each circled word on the lines below.

The magority of people who have seen the Muppets can appreciate the talent of the late Jim Henson. He and the people who worked with him made puppetry a jenuine art form. Miss Piggy, Cookie Monster, Kermit, and the other Muppets are known for their unique personalities. Within their korus of voices, the calm, frantik, grouchy, and gealous personalities are easy to distinguish.

Although Henson was born in Mississippi, he grew up in the visinity of Washington, D.C. His interest in theater began in high school, where his urje to act led him to take part in school plays. A talented artist, Henson also worked on scenery desin. As a boy, he loved listening to Charlie McCarthy, a ventriloquist's dummy on a popular radio show. In the 1950s, Henson's attention turned to television. He often said he owed a det of gratitude to the *Kukla, Fran, and Ollie* show. Watching it made him realize that he wanted to gain nowledge of puppetry teknique. Henson took a university course on that subject. Then during a trip to Europe, he spent hours watching puppet shows, many of which were based on local foklore.

Henson made an important chareer choice—he decided to fokus his enerjy on hand puppets. He and a friend created a show for a local TV station. They probably never imagined what a jigantic success one frog-like karacter would become. In an insident that has become a lejend, Henson asked for his mother's concent to cut up her old green coat. Can you guess what he used it for?

1. _____
2. _____
3. _____
4. _____
5. _____
6. _____
7. _____
8. _____
9. _____
10. _____
11. _____
12. _____
13. _____
14. _____
15. _____
16. _____
17. _____
18. _____
19. _____
20. _____

Spelling Power

Spelling Power

Lesson 9: Spelling the Schwa Sound

Word Bank

beautiful	ignorant	compliment	museum	desperate
personal	error	stirrup	hibernate	temporary

Key Concept

The schwa (ə) stands for an unstressed vowel sound. Any unstressed vowel may spell the schwa sound. As you learn to spell the words with unstressed syllables, try to visualize the words.

above   item   visible   gallon   cactus

Spelling Practice

Choose the word from the Word Bank that matches each pronunciation. Circle the vowels that spell the schwa sound. Remember the schwa sound can only appear in unaccented syllables.

Example: \viz'ə bəl\   visible

1. \er'ər\   _____

2. \stur'əp\   _____

3. \tem'pə rer'ē   _____

4. \mū zē'əm\   _____

5. \bū'ti fəl\   _____

6. \com'plə mənt\   _____

7. \des'pər it\   _____

8. \hī'bər nāt'\   _____

9. \ig'nər ənt\   _____

10. \pur'sən əl\   _____

Spelling in Context

Write the word from the Word Bank that best fits each sentence.

1. When I visited the stable, I was _____ to conceal how little I knew about horses.

2. I didn't want the riding teacher to think I was _____ or clumsy.

3. As the teacher showed how to adjust a _____, I watched carefully.

LESSON 9 continued

4. Hoping the teacher would _____ me on my expertise, I tried to impress her.

5. "Do horses _____ in the winter?" I asked casually.

Proofreading Practice

Read the paragraph below. Find the five misspelled words and circle them. Then, on the numbered lines, write the correct spelling for each circled word.

How did the earliest humans live? Museam exhibits offer clues. For example, Neanderthals crafted a variety of flint tools. They built temperary shelters of animal hides stretched over frames. They polished ivory for personol ornaments. They surrounded their dead with beautyful flowers. Clearly it would be an errer to think of these early humans as savages.

1. _____   **3.** _____   **5.** _____

2. _____   **4.** _____

Spelling Application

Listed below are six more words that reflect the Key Concepts you have learned.

abacus   admiral   cavern
minimum   versatile   wonderful

Write each word below and then divide each word into syllables. You may use a dictionary for help.

1. _____   **4.** _____

2. _____   **5.** _____

3. _____   **6.** _____

Now use the six words to complete the imaginary book titles.

7. *The* _____ *Vegetable Diet,* by Cole Slaugh and B. Russell Sproutz

8. *The Admirable* _____, by H. E. Row

9. *Math with a* _____ *of Effort,* by Cal Q. Later

10. *Excavating the Deepest* _____, by Doug A. Pitt

11. *Our* _____ *Backpacking Trip,* by Walker Soxoff and Bliss Terz

12. *How to Use an* _____, by Count Ollie D'Beeds

Spelling Power

Lesson 10: Spelling the \ô\ Sound

Word Bank

launch	applaud	awesome	stalwart	naughty
author	caution	awkwardly	warrior	daughter

Key Concepts

1. In many words, the \ô\ sound is spelled *au* or *aw*.

August   fault   awful   drawn

2. In some words, the \ô\ sound is spelled *a, augh,* or *ough*.

halt   taught   ought

Spelling Practice

Put the words from the Word Bank in alphabetical order. Circle the letters that spell the \ô\ sound in each word.

1. _____
2. _____
3. _____
4. _____
5. _____
6. _____
7. _____
8. _____
9. _____
10. _____

Spelling in Context

Write the words from the Word Bank that best complete each sentence.

1. We gathered around the TV to watch the _____ of the space shuttle.

2. Thanks to the _____ of careful engineers, everything went smoothly.

3. The rocket rising into the morning sky was an _____ sight.

4. The neighbors' five-year-old _____ stood staring at the screen.

5. As the rocket rose, she began to _____.

LESSON 10 continued

Proofreading Practice

Read the paragraph below. Find the five misspelled words and circle them. Then, on the numbered lines, write the correct spelling for each circled word.

   Born fifteen hundred years ago, al-Khansa was the dotter of one waurrior and the sister of another. She was also the awthor of some of the Arab world's earliest poetry. Members of her tribe gathered to applod her. They thought her work would bring them immortality. Time has proven them right. Her poem for her staulwart brother, killed in battle, still touches readers today.

1. _____ 3. _____ 5. _____

2. _____ 4. _____

Spelling Application

Listed below are eight more words that reflect the Key Concepts you have learned.

bought   caught   defraud   falter
haughty   thoughtless   vault   yawning

Circle the letters that spell the \ô\ sound in each word. Then write the words that best complete each Tom Swiftie pun below.

1. "How _____ of me. I forgot to put the car in gear," said Tom shiftlessly.

2. "The gymnasts are going to _____ right over me," said Tom understandingly.

3. "The other runners are starting to _____. I think I can sprint ahead," said Tom racily.

4. "Look at all the hay I just _____!" said Tom balefully.

5. "The river has cut quite a _____ chasm," said Tom gorgeously.

6. "I've often _____ up with that tired old horse," said Tom naggingly.

7. "I've made a devious plan to _____ people," said Tom stingingly.

8. "Just tell that _____ young lady to follow me," said Tom misleadingly.

Spelling Power

Lesson 11: Spelling the \or\ Sound

Word Bank

escort	ordinary	courtyard	hoarse	quarrel
ornamental	mourn	concourse	uproar	quarantine

Key Concepts

1. Usually the \or\ sound is spelled *or, our,* or *oar.*

h<u>or</u>n   c<u>our</u>t   s<u>oar</u>

2. After *qu,* the \or\ sound is spelled *ar.*

qu<u>ar</u>t   qu<u>ar</u>ry

Spelling Practice

Put the words from the Word Bank in alphabetical order. Circle the letters that spell the \or\ sound in each word.

1. _____
2. _____
3. _____
4. _____
5. _____
6. _____
7. _____
8. _____
9. _____
10. _____

Spelling in Context

Write the word from the Word Bank that best completes each sentence. Pay special attention to the letters that spell the \or\ sound.

1. We visited the new community _____ near City Hall yesterday.

2. Its sunny _____ was filled with blossoming cherry trees.

3. Hand-painted _____ tiles brightened the walkways.

4. Our guide had a cold, so his voice was _____.

5. We watched pigeons _____ over crumbs from our picnic lunch.

LESSON 11 continued

Proofreading Practice

Read the paragraph below. Find the five misspelled words and circle them. Then, on the numbered lines, write the correct spelling for each circled word.

The year was 1348. Venice was in an upror. Half the populace was ill, and a strict quorantine was in effect. No one could enter or leave the city without an escourt. This was no oardinary epidemic; this was the dreaded plague. So many people had died that few were left to moarn the dead. People thought that "bad vapors" spread the disease. No one guessed the true culprit: a virus carried by fleas found on the city's many rats.

1. _____   3. _____   5. _____

2. _____   4. _____

Spelling Application

Listed below are eight more words that reflect the Key Concepts you have learned. Circle the letters that spell the \or\ sound in each word.

clipboard	coarse	forty	fourteen
majority	pour	quartet	quartz

Choose the words that best answer the riddles. Write your choices on the lines.

1. I'm what rain does during storms. What am I? _____

2. I'm a stone with crystal forms. What am I? _____

3. I'm the opposite of *fine*. What am I? _____

4. I come after thirty-nine. What am I? _____

5. I'm needed by politicians. What am I? _____

6. I may include four musicians. What am I? _____

7. I'm one half of twenty-eight. What am I? _____

8. I'm used as a writing board. What am I? _____

Spelling Power

Lesson 12: Doubling the Final Consonant

Word Bank

shipment	flatly	admits	omits	expels
shipper	flatten	admittance	omitting	expelled

Key Concepts

Many words end in a c-v-c (consonant-vowel-consonant) pattern:

c v c	c v c
s h i p	f r e t

1. When adding a suffix starting with a vowel to a one-syllable c-v-c word, double the final consonant:

   ship + er = shipper   fret + ed = fretted

2. When adding a suffix starting with a consonant to any c-v-c word, do not double the final consonant:

   ship + ment = shipment   fret + ful = fretful   regret + ful = regretful

3. For c-v-c words of more than one syllable, double the final consonant only if the word's last syllable is stressed:

   regret' + ing = regretting   regret' + able = regrettable

   (but: mar'vel + ing = marveling   mar'vel + ous = marvelous)

Spelling Practice

Choose the words from the Word Bank that combine the word roots and suffixes shown. Write your choices on the lines. Then write the number of the Key Concept that applies to each choice.

Example: fret + ed = _____fretted 1_____

1. ship + er = _____
2. admit + s = _____
3. ship + ment = _____
4. flat + en = _____
5. omit + ing = _____

6. expel + s = _____
7. flat + ly = _____
8. admit + ance = _____
9. expel + ed = _____
10. omit + s = _____

Spelling in Context

Write the word from the Word Bank that best completes each sentence.

1. Dana's teacher _____ each student's lowest test score when figuring grades.

2. At her school, students who break rules may be _____.

3. The principal _____ that the school's policy is strict.

LESSON 12 continued

4. Teachers _____ refuse to change the policy.

5. Students there behave so well that the school _____ only one or two students per year.

Proofreading Practice

Read the paragraph below. Find the five misspelled words and circle them. Then, on the numbered lines, write the correct spelling for each circled word.

The shippment—jars of fine Greek olive oil—came from early Rome. The shiper had hoped to find wealth in the markets of Carthage, in northern Africa. Omiting sufficient preparations for foul weather, he soon found disaster. A storm churned up to flaten his vessels, sending them to the Mediterranean Sea floor. Two thousand years later divers located the wreckage and gained admitance to the crumbling cargo holds.

1. _____   **3.** _____   **5.** _____

2. _____   **4.** _____

Spelling Application

Below are eight words and suffixes that reflect the Key Concepts from this lesson. Add the suffixes to the words. Use the Key Concepts to decide whether or not to double the final consonants. After each word, write the number of the Key Concept that applies.

beginner	commitment	forgetful	rebellion
recurrence	strapping	submits	unwrapped

1. unwrap + ed = _____

2. rebel + ion = _____

3. recur + ence = _____

4. submit + s = _____

5. strap + ing = _____

6. commit + ment = _____

7. forget + ful = _____

8. begin + er = _____

Spelling Power

Unit 3 Review
Lessons 9–12

admittance	author	awkwardly	compliment	courtyard
daughter	error	expels	flatten	hibernate
museum	ordinary	ornamental	omits	personal
quarantine	shipper	stirrup	uproar	warrior

Fill in the crossword puzzle using words from the list above.

Across
3. a place where art or artifacts can be seen
6. leaves out
7. private; relating to an individual
8. one experienced in battle
9. for decoration
12. writer
13. forcefully pushes out
15. to be inactive for the winter
16. a mistake
17. female child
18. foot ring on a saddle
19. enclosed patio
20. of common quality; usual

Down
1. restriction to keep illness from spreading
2. praise
4. noisy confusion
5. to knock over; to make flat
10. an antonym for *gracefully*
11. entry
14. one who sends cargo

Name _____ Date _____ Class _____

Spelling Power

Proofreading Application

Lessons 9–12
Read the modernized fairy tale below. Find the twenty misspelled review words and circle them.
Then, on the numbered lines, write the correct spelling for each circled word.

Little Red Riding Hood

Once there was a little girl named Red Riding Hood. Her parents, Mr. and Mrs. Hood, owned a market near the town concorse. Every Tuesday they received a shippment of oranges, and Red always took some to her grandmother. A neighbor would escourt Red, for cawtion was needed in the dangerous forest. One Tuesday the neighbor was away on temperary business. Unafraid, the staulwart Red ventured into the forest alone.

Unfortunately the local Big Bad Wolf had grown desperite for a meal and had decided that Red's grandmother would make a perfect snack. On his way to the condo where Red's grandmother lived, he happened to see Red with a basket of oranges. "Awsome!" he chortled. "Double serving for me." He rushed to the grandmother's house and swallowed her whole, omiting even the brushing of his teeth. Then, clad in one of the grandmother's nightgowns, he settled down to wait for Red.

The girl soon arrived. "I have a cold," moaned the disguised wolf in a hourse voice. "Come closer, Dear."

Red, who was far from ignerant, flattly refused. She had noticed her grandmother's beautyful pearl earring stuck between the wolf's fangs. The wolf tried to lawnch himself at her, but Red was on her school wrestling team. She promptly placed the creature in a headlock. "Naugty wolf!" she scolded. "Give Grandma back!"

"Never!" howled the wolf, clamping his jaws tightly shut.

"At least he admitts he swallowed her," thought Red. "Come on—don't quorrel," she urged, tickling his paws. He laughed so hard that he expeled Grandma, who grabbed her earring as she shot out of his mouth.

"I applod you, Red!" exclaimed Grandma. The girl beamed with joy. Not even the wolf could moarn for long.

"She gave me heartburn," he admitted, helping himself to an orange. "I should have made her take off those spike-heeled shoes."

1. _____ 8. _____ 15. _____
2. _____ 9. _____ 16. _____
3. _____ 10. _____ 17. _____
4. _____ 11. _____ 18. _____
5. _____ 12. _____ 19. _____
6. _____ 13. _____ 20. _____
7. _____ 14. _____

Spelling Power

Spelling Power

Lesson 13: The \ou\ and \oi\ Sounds

Word Bank

destroy	poison	disappoint	announce	powerful
loyal	rejoice	discount	surround	allowance

Key Concepts

1. The vowel sound \ou\ can be spelled *ou* or *ow*.

   st<u>ou</u>t   cl<u>ow</u>n

2. The vowel sound \oi\ can be spelled *oi* or *oy*.

   c<u>oi</u>n   j<u>oy</u>ous

Spelling Practice

Write each word from the Word Bank in the appropriate column. Circle the letters that make the designated sound.

Words with the \ou\ sound:

1. _____
2. _____
3. _____
4. _____
5. _____

Words with the \oi\ sound:

6. _____
7. _____
8. _____
9. _____
10. _____

Spelling in Context

Choose the word from the Word Bank that best completes each sentence. Write your choices on the lines.

1. A strong and _____ queen ruled England for many years.

2. She was able to _____ herself with sensible advisors.

3. Her advisors received a generous _____ for living expenses.

4. The advisors worked on plans to _____ enemy camps.

5. Some enemies spread rumors to _____ the people's minds against the queen.

LESSON 13 continued

Proofreading Practice

As you read the following advertisement, circle the five misspelled words. Write the correct spelling for each circled word on the lines below.

An Invitation for Our Loial Customers

We are happy to annownce our anniversary celebration. Come and rejoyce with us on our tenth year in business! No fooling—on April 1 you can receive a 20 percent discownt on everything you buy. We have lots of merchandise in stock, so we will not disappoynt you. Free gifts and refreshments for everybody!

1. _____   3. _____   5. _____

2. _____   4. _____

Spelling Application

Below are ten more words that reflect the Key Concepts you have learned. Find and circle each word in the word maze. Then write the words on the lines. For each word, circle the letters that spell the \oi\ or \ou\ sound.

annoy	devour	employ	joyful	noisy
plow	pouch	prowler	scout	soil

```
J Y T W O L P
O O S U Y R N
Y L O X O H O
F P I W N C I
U M L E N U S
L E M T A O Y
R U O L E P A
A D E V O U R
```

1. _____   6. _____

2. _____   7. _____

3. _____   8. _____

4. _____   9. _____

5. _____   10. _____

Spelling Power

Lesson 14: Words with *ie* and *ei*

Word Bank

thief	fiercely	weight	receiver	leisure
wield	conscience	reign	counterfeit	deceit

Key Concepts

1. Remember this rhyme to help you spell many words with the *ie* and *ei* combinations.

Write i *before* e	shield	relief
except after c,	receipt	ceiling
or when sounded as a,		
as in neighbor *and* weigh.		

2. Memorize these exceptions:

conscience	leisure	seize
either	neither	weird
forfeit	foreign	

Spelling Practice

Write the words from the Word Bank in the correct columns.

Words with *ie*

1. _____
2. _____
3. _____
4. _____

Words with *ei*

5. _____
6. _____
7. _____
8. _____
9. _____
10. _____

Spelling in Context

Choose the word from the Word Bank that best completes each sentence. Write your choices on the lines.

1. The art criminal was a master of _____.

2. His warehouses held museum pieces worth their _____ in gold.

3. He served as the _____ of paintings that his cohorts stole.

4. He was a forger as well as a _____.

5. He created _____ works nearly identical to the originals.

LESSON 14 continued

Proofreading Practice

Read the paragraph below. Find the five misspelled words and circle them. Then, on the numbered lines, write the correct spelling for each circled word.

What's the world's oldest written story? It may be the *Epic of Gilgamesh*, the tale of a Sumerian king. The riegn of the real Gilgamesh began around 2600 B.C. The epic blends legend and fact. In the epic, Gilgamesh can weild mighty weapons and wrestle lions with his bare hands. Yet he also has a consceince and a love of beauty. He stays feircely loyal to a childhood friend. In his liesure time, he enjoys fine arts.

1. _____   3. _____   5. _____

2. _____   4. _____

Spelling Application

Listed below are eight more words that reflect the Key Concepts you have learned. Circle the *ie* or *ei* in each word.

believe   conceited   eighty   freight
pierce   priest   seize   yield

Use the words to complete the analogies below. Pay special attention to the *ie* and *ei* patterns.

1. laugh : cry :: _____ : doubt

2. _____ : grasp :: smile : grin

3. puncture : _____ :: astonish : surprise

4. law : attorney :: religion : _____

5. brave : cowardly :: _____ : humble

6. relinquish : _____ :: conceal : hide

7. _____ : cargo :: flower : blossom

8. four : sixteen :: twenty : _____

Spelling Power

Lesson 15: Dropping the Final Silent e

Word Bank

debatable	contributor	probably	relating	rosy
believable	navigator	horribly	acquiring	spicy

Key Concepts

For words ending in silent *e*:

1. Drop the *e* to add a suffix starting with a vowel.
   debate + able = debatable   urge + ent = urgent
   file + ing = filing

2. Drop the *e* to add *y*.
   sauce + y = saucy   nose + y = nosy

3. To add *-ly* to a word ending in *le*, usually drop the *le*.
   able + ly = ably

Spelling Practice

Write the words from the Word Bank that combine the word roots and suffixes below.

1. relate + ing = _____

2. navigate + or = _____

3. debate + able = _____

4. probable + ly = _____

5. rose + y = _____

6. spice + y = _____

7. contribute + or = _____

8. believe + able = _____

9. horrible + ly = _____

10. acquire + ing = _____

Spelling in Context

Write the word from the Word Bank that best completes each sentence.

1. For only a few dollars, you can become a _____ to our school jog-a-thon.

2. We're earning money for field trips and activities _____ to our studies.

3. This may not be _____, but last year one girl jogged more than ten miles.

4. It's _____ whether anyone can beat her record.

5. The effort didn't seem _____ difficult for her; she was out of breath, but smiling.

LESSON 15 continued

Proofreading Practice

Read the paragraph below. Find the five misspelled words and circle them. Then, on the numbered lines, write the correct spelling for each circled word.

Do you like jalapeño peppers? These spicey snacks are guaranteed to make your face turn rosey. Hot peppers were grown in Mesoamerica as early as 5000 B.C. They were probabley brought back to Europe by Christopher Colombus or by another navigateor of the same period. Acquireing a taste for jalapeños takes patience—and plenty of ice water—but fans say it's worth the effort!

1. _____   3. _____   5. _____

2. _____   4. _____

Spelling Application

Below are eight more words that reflect the Key Concepts you have learned. Combine the word roots with the suffixes shown. Write your answers on the lines. Then use the numbered letters to finish the quip at the bottom of the page.

confidence	intensely	juicy	politest
refining	rehearsal	terribly	translator

1. confide + ence = _ _ _ _ _ _ _ _ _ _

                8

5. intense + ly = _ _ _ _ _ _ _ _ _

              3

2. terrible + ly = _ _ _ _ _ _ _ _

            7

6. polite + est = _ _ _ _ _ _ _ _

           4

3. juice + y = _ _ _ _ _

      2

7. rehearse + al = _ _ _ _ _ _ _ _

            1

4. translate + or = _ _ _ _ _ _ _ _ _ _

            5

8. refine + ing = _ _ _ _ _ _ _

           6

Old kangaroos never die; they just

_ _ _   _ _ _   _ _   _ _ _ _ _ s.
1 2 3   4 2 5   4 6   7 4 2 3 8

Spelling Power

Lesson 16: Keeping the Final Silent e

Word Bank

excitement	merely	changeable	outrageous	hoeing
tasteful	hopeless	peaceable	agreeing	gleeful

Key Concepts

For words that end in silent e:

1. Keep the e when adding a suffix starting with a consonant.

spit<u>e</u> + <u>f</u>ul = spiteful

ama<u>ze</u> + <u>ment</u> = amazement

Two exceptions: *judge + ment = judgment*
awe + ful = awful

2. Some words end in *ee* or *oe*. Keep the final *e* when adding any suffix to these words.

fr<u>ee</u> + dom = fr<u>ee</u>dom   fr<u>ee</u> + ing = fr<u>ee</u>ing

sh<u>oe</u> + ing = sh<u>oe</u>ing

3. Some words end in *c* or *g* + silent *e*. Keep the *e* when adding a suffix starting with a consonant or with the vowel *a* or *o*.

pea<u>ce</u> + <u>f</u>ul = peaceful

enlar<u>ge</u> + <u>ment</u> = enlargement

tra<u>ce</u> + able = tra<u>ce</u>able

coura<u>ge</u> + <u>ous</u> = coura<u>ge</u>ous

Spelling Practice

Choose the words from the Word Bank that combine the word roots and suffixes shown. Write your choices on the lines. Then write the number of the Key Concept that applies to each word.

Example: amaze + ment = _____amazement 1_____

1. agree + ing = _____

2. change + able = _____

3. excite + ment = _____

4. glee + ful = _____

5. hoe + ing = _____

6. hope + less = _____

7. mere + ly = _____

8. outrage + ous = _____

9. peace + able = _____

10. taste + ful = _____

Spelling in Context

Write the word from the Word Bank that best completes each sentence.

1. What's the wildest, most _____ gift you've ever received?

2. For me, it was a chameleon, a lizard with _____ skin colors and patterns.

3. My brother's grin showed that he was _____ about my new pet, but my parents'
response was another matter.

LESSON 16 continued

4. They ordered me to get rid of the lizard; the situation seemed _____.

5. To my surprise, after a week they were cheerfully _____ to let me keep the chameleon.

Proofreading Practice

Read the paragraph below. Find the five misspelled words and circle them. Then, on the numbered lines, write the correct spelling for each circled word.

Wow—you're back in 2500 B.C.! A time machine has whisked you to the Indus Valley in India. Filled with excitment, you begin to look around. You see farmers hoing ground for crops of barley, wheat, and melons. Ahead you see not merly a village, but a well-planned city. Here in Mohenjo-Daro, 40,000 peacable citizens live in houses with bathrooms and sewer systems. Jewelers craft tastful necklaces of gems and gold. A written language records events. This culture is far from primitive.

1. _____ 3. _____ 5. _____

2. _____ 4. _____

Spelling Application

Below are eight more words that reflect the Key Concepts you have learned. Use the words to complete the "terse verse" rhymes below. You will use two of the words in the last rhyme.

bravely	canoeing	ceaseless	forceful
grateful	overseeing	refereeing	statement

1. glad to have food: _____ for a plateful

2. bragging while _____: gloating while boating

3. _____ but incorrect: strong but wrong

4. _____ supply of pasta: steady spaghetti

5. make a _____ about a cat's leap: announce a pounce

6. show scorn _____: sneer without fear

7. supervising the umpires' actions: _____ the _____

Name _____ Date_____ Class _____

Spelling Power

Unit 4 Review
Lessons 13–16

agreeing	allowance	changeable	conscience	counterfeit
debatable	disappoint	gleeful	horribly	navigator
outrageous	peaceable	poison	reign	relating
rosy	spicy	surround	thief	wield

Choose the words from the list above that best complete the sentences. Write your choices on the lines.

1. During the _____ of Elizabeth I, England and Spain vied for mastery of the seas.

2. Francis Drake, an expert English _____, explored the uncharted waters of the New World.

3. He could _____ a sword as well as he could sail.

4. His knowledge of the shifting, _____ winds helped him to defeat the Spanish Armada.

5. The heavy Spanish ships could not _____ Drake's small but speedy fleet.

6. The Spanish called him a pirate and a _____, but the English called him a hero.

7. Drake clearly had a _____, for he always treated his prisoners kindly.

8. Drake's crew knew him as a _____ man, slow to anger and calm in a crisis.

9. After Queen Elizabeth knighted Drake, his future looked _____ and bright.

10. Drake's nephew wrote a book _____ Drake's many adventures.

Unscramble the letters to spell the review words defined below. Write the unscrambled words on the lines. Use the word list to check your spelling.

11. psyci _____ peppery; flavorful
12. osnoip _____ a deadly substance
13. flegule _____ merry; joyful
14. brilohry _____ in a dreadful way
15. erggaine _____ consenting; being in accord
16. labbadeet _____ open to discussion
17. wealcanol _____ money or consideration granted
18. tinpasodip _____ to fail to live up to expectations
19. sootguarue _____ extreme; disgraceful
20. tofeecinrut _____ forged; fake

Spelling Power

Proofreading Application

Lessons 13–16

Read the Tom Swiftie puns below. Find the twenty misspelled review words and circle them. Then, on the numbered lines, write the correct spelling for each circled word.

1. "That's a fast and pouwerful train," said Tom expressively.
2. "Rejoyce! Our team is going to the playoffs!" said Tom winsomely.
3. "The suspect's alibi isn't believeable; pat him down for weapons," said Tom friskily.
4. "Tigers attack fiercly, so we have to restrain them," said Tom cagily.
5. "Merly seeing that big piano makes me happy," said Tom grandly.
6. "I'm acquireing a new pair of sunglasses," said Tom shadily.
7. "We need more wieght at the back of the boat!" said Tom sternly.
8. "I'm a contributeor to the animal shelter," said Tom pettily.
9. "I'll always be loial to the Navy," said Tom fleetingly.
10. "Let me annownce that I'll be living in a new place soon," said Tom movingly.
11. "I'm probablely going to pitch for the softball team," said Tom underhandedly.
12. "No earthquake will ever destroi this city," said Tom faultlessly.
13. "This is hopeless; the worm keeps falling off my fishhook," said Tom debatably.
14. "I'm a master of deciet; I just told another fib," said Tom reliably.
15. "You left big chunks of soil where you were hoing," said Tom cloddishly.
16. "When this rings, you have to pick up the reciever and say 'Hello,'" said Tom phonily.
17. "In my liesure time, I play chess and backgammon," said Tom gamely.
18. "Why all the excitement about my barbecue recipe?" asked Tom saucily.
19. "I think my orange, red, and purple shirt is quite tastful," said Tom loudly.
20. "I'll give you a discownt on a tool for gathering leaves," said Tom rakishly.

1. _____	8. _____	15. _____
2. _____	9. _____	16. _____
3. _____	10. _____	17. _____
4. _____	11. _____	18. _____
5. _____	12. _____	19. _____
6. _____	13. _____	20. _____
7. _____	14. _____	

Spelling Power

Lesson 17: Keeping the Final *y*

Word Bank

alleys	highways	buoyed	dismayed	surveyor
playful	dignifying	relaying	payment	enjoyment

Key Concepts

1. If a word ends in a vowel + *y*, keep the *y* when adding a suffix.

   play + ful = playful   joy + ous = joyous
   relay + s = relays

2. To add *-ing* to any word ending in *y*, keep the *y*.

   play + ing = playing   pry + ing = prying
   deny + ing = denying

Spelling Practice

Put the words from the Word Bank in alphabetical order. After each word, write the number of the Key Concept that applies to it. Then circle the vowel + *y* in each word that includes that combination.

1. _____
2. _____
3. _____
4. _____
5. _____

6. _____
7. _____
8. _____
9. _____
10. _____

Spelling in Context

In the paragraph below, write the word from the Word Bank that is a synonym for each word or phrase in parentheses.

I was nervous about babysitting, but the thought of earning money (lifted) _____ my spirits. How hard could a few hours with a (fun-loving) _____ two-year-old be? I soon found out. "Funny? Funny?" he asked, pouring shampoo all over the living room. Not (honoring) _____ his question with a reply, I began cleaning. I was (taken aback) _____ to learn how much work childcare is. I am (passing along) _____ my story as a warning: Look before you leap.

LESSON 17 continued

Proofreading Practice

Read the paragraph below. Find the five misspelled words and circle them. Then, on the numbered lines, write the correct spelling for each circled word.

The Maya are a New World mystery. This culture began its rise around 300 B.C. A surveior must have laid out each Maya city, for temples, homes, streets, and alleis followed careful patterns. Broad plazas provided space for enjoiment during festivals. Highwaies between cities encouraged trade. Maya writings show that the cities warred, and the victors demanded paiment of goods and prisoners. Around 900 A.D., all the cities were abandoned. What happened? No one knows.

1. _____   3. _____   5. _____

2. _____   4. _____

Spelling Application

Listed below are six more words that reflect the Key Concepts you have learned.

boyish   destroyed   displaying   holidays   replying   valleys

Do you speak Pig Latin? In this made-up "language," you take away the first letter from the beginning of a word. You then add the letter to an extra syllable at the end. For example, *pig* becomes *ig-pay*. *Latin* becomes *Atin-Lay*.

"Translate" each Pig Latin word below. To check your work, put together the word roots and suffixes in parentheses.

1. oyish-bay _____ (boy + ish)

2. alleys-vay _____ (valley + s)

3. eplying-ray _____ (reply + ing)

4. isplaying-day _____ (display + ing)

5. olidays-hay _____ (holiday + s)

6. estroyed-day _____ (destroy + ed)

Spelling Power

Lesson 18: Changing y to i

Word Bank

replied	laziness	denial	easier	envies
rallied	friendliness	ordinarily	funniest	pharmacies

Key Concepts

For words ending in a consonant + y:

1. Change the y to i before adding a suffix:

pry + ed = pried   fancy + ful = fanciful

rely + ance = reliance

2. To form a plural noun or to form the present tense of a verb, change the y to i and add es.

enemy → enemies   ·   deny → denies

Spelling Practice

Choose the word from the Word Bank that is formed from each word root below. Write your choices on the lines.

1. deny _____

2. easy _____

3. envy _____

4. friendly _____

5. funny _____

6. lazy _____

7. ordinary _____

8. pharmacy _____

9. rally _____

10. reply _____

Spelling in Context

Write the word from the Word Bank that best completes each sentence.

1. When our club president suggested a service project, we all _____ to the cause faithfully.

2. We asked local merchants if they needed help, and many _____ that they did.

3. One merchant said no, but we didn't take his _____ seriously.

4. Two _____ and a grocery store asked us to deliver orders to homebound customers.

5. The mayor gave us a service award, and now everyone at school _____ us.

LESSON 18 continued

Proofreading Practice

Read the paragraph below. Find the five misspelled words and circle them. Then, on the numbered lines, write the correct spelling for each circled word.

What was the funnyest comic strip of the 1950s? It may well have been *Pogo*, by Walt Kelly. Pogo Possum, known for his friendlyness, lived in the Okefenokee Swamp. Albert Alligator, known for his lazyness, was Pogo's toothy sidekick. Though alligators ordinaryly eat opossums, Albert found peanut-butter sandwiches easyer to digest. The antics of this unlikely pair show the art of cartooning at its best.

1. _____   3. _____   5. _____

2. _____   4. _____

Spelling Application

Below are eight more words to help you practice the Key Concepts you have learned. Join the word roots and suffixes or form the plurals, as indicated. Then check your spelling by using the box to decode the correct answers. For example, 21-42-54 would be FRY.

amplified   chilliness   hobbies   lonelier
modify   reliable   strategies   thrifty

	1	2	3	4	5
1	A	B	C	D	E
2	F	G	H	I,J	K
3	L	M	N	O	P
4	Q	R	S	T	U
5	V	W	X	Y	Z

1. lonely + er = _____ 31-34-33-15-31-24-15-42

2. thrifty + est = _____ 44-23-42-24-21-44-24-15-43-44

3. hobby (plural form) = _____ 23-34-12-12-24-15-43

4. chilly + ness = _____ 13-23-24-31-31-24-33-15-43-43

5. modify + er = _____ 32-34-14-24-21-24-15-42

6. amplify + ed = _____ 11-32-35-31-24-21-24-15-14

7. rely + able = _____ 42-15-31-24-11-12-31-15

8. strategy (plural form) = _____ 43-44-42-11-44-15-22-24-15-43

Spelling Power

Lesson 19: The Suffix -ous

Word Bank

courteous	ruinous	furious	venomous	ambitious
miraculous	luscious	luxurious	numerous	victorious

Key Concepts

1. Many adjectives use the suffix -ous, meaning "having the qualities of."

   courage<u>ous</u>   nutriti<u>ous</u>   graci<u>ous</u>

2. Some word roots change their form when adding -ous.

   fame + ous = famous   glory + ous = glorious

   ambition + ous = ambitious

   miracle + ous = miraculous

3. Some adjectives that use -ous do not have familiar word roots.

   precious   obvious

Spelling Practice

Write the adjectives from the Word Bank that originate from the words below. Mark * after each adjective whose word root changed form when -ous was added.

1. ruin _____
2. venom _____
3. fury _____
4. luxury _____
5. victory _____

6. ambition _____
7. courtesy _____
8. number _____
9. miracle _____

Write the remaining listed adjective, whose word root is not familiar.

10. _____

Spelling in Context

Write the words from the Word Bank that best complete the sentences.

1. Mimi and Pizarro vacationed in splendor on a _____ cruise ship.

2. Mimi, always polite, remained _____ when a steward spilled tomato juice on her evening gown.

3. The hot-tempered Pizarro got _____ and challenged the steward to a duel.

LESSON 19 continued

4. Pizarro and the steward would toss banana cream pies at each other from fifty paces; the dueler who was

_____ would receive a dozen pies as his prize.

5. Mimi pointed out that victory would be _____ to the portly Pizarro's diet.

Proofreading Practice

Read the paragraph below. Find the five misspelled words and circle them. Then, on the numbered lines, write the correct spelling for each circled word.

S-s-snakes! Harmless or venomus, common or rare, these reptiles catch our attention. They come in numerus types. They can live in the driest deserts and the wettest jungles. In India, cobras perform for ambitius snake charmers. In China, some diners consider python a luscius treat. In several Native American cultures, rattlesnakes have been considered miraculis gods. We humans may love snakes or hate them, but we seldom ignore them.

1. _____   **3.** _____   **5.** _____

2. _____   **4.** _____

Spelling Application

Listed below are six more words that reflect the Key Concepts you have learned.

anxious curious delicious   obvious previoussuspicious

Write each word vertically. Then make an acrostic for each word. Each term in your acrostic must relate to the meaning of the vertical word.

Example: famous
f ans
a pplause
m uch-admired
o utstanding
u nequaled
s tar

1.   **3.**   **5.**

2.   **4.**   **6.**

Spelling Power

Lesson 20: The Suffix -ion

Word Bank

| application | exception | portion | conviction | tension |
| revolution | suspicion | tradition | intrusion | permission |

Key Concepts

The suffix -ion, meaning "act of" or "state of," marks nouns.

1. Nouns with -ion end in one of two ways: -tion or -sion.

   rela<u>tion</u>   corre<u>ction</u>   ten<u>sion</u>   confu<u>sion</u>

   (Only one English noun ends in -cion: suspi<u>cion</u>.)

2. Since -tion and -sion sound the same, you need to memorize the spellings of -ion nouns. Try to visualize these words as you learn them.

3. Many word roots change form when -ion is added.

   decide + ion = decision
   intrude + ion = intrusion
   receive + ion = reception
   permit + ion = permission

4. Some -ion nouns have no familiar word root.

   motion   condition

Spelling Practice

Choose the noun from the Word Bank that originates from each word below. Write your choices on the lines. Mark * after nouns whose bases changed form when -ion was added.

Nouns with -tion

1. convict _____

2. except _____

3. apply _____

4. revolve _____

Nouns with -sion

5. tense _____

6. intrude _____

7. permit _____

Write the listed word that ends in -cion.

8. _____

Write the remaining two words.

9. _____   10. _____

Spelling in Context

Write the words from the Word Bank that best complete the sentences.

1. _____ ran high as we pleaded to visit Whirl-a-World theme park.

2. Its roller coaster, the Planetary Plunger, makes a 360-degree _____ around a neon "sun."

LESSON 20 continued

3. We argued with _____ that we would behave responsibly.

4. We agreed to pay a large _____ of the costs.

5. At last, we won our parents' _____ to go.

Proofreading Practice

Read the paragraph below. Find the five misspelled words and circle them. Then, on the numbered lines, write the correct spelling for each circled word.

Annie Elizabeth Delany was the excepsion to many a rule. She was the first African American woman to attend dental school at Columbia University. Her entrance applicacion caused a furor. By tradision, only whites were accepted. She was viewed with suspition, and her presence was seen as an intrution. She refused to back down. After graduating in 1923, Dr. Delany became one of only two African American dentists practicing in New York City.

1. _____ **3.** _____ **5.** _____

2. _____ **4.** _____

Spelling Application

Listed below are eight more nouns that reflect the Key Concepts you have learned.

admission	commotion	competition	determination
generation	impression	profession	promotion

Use these nouns to complete the rhymed definitions below. Circle the *-tion* or *-sion* in each noun that you write.

1. A contest might be called a _____.

2. An entrance fee is "the price of _____."

3. When you don't give up, you show _____.

4. Your age-mates are your _____.

5. A big fuss is known as a _____.

6. Advancing to the next grade is a _____.

7. A career can be known as a _____.

8. To be hired, you must make a good _____.

Spelling Power

Unit 5 Review

Lessons 17–20

alleys	application	conviction	dignifying	dismayed
enjoyment	envies	exception	friendliness	intrusion
miraculous	numerous	ordinarily	portion	rallied
replied	ruinous	surveyor	venomous	victorious

Choose the words from the list above that best complete the sentences. Write your choices on the lines.

1. For pure pleasure and _____, read *Old Possum's Book of Practical Cats*, by T. S. Eliot.

2. His humorous poems tell of cats living in various locations, from fine mansions to lowly back _____.

3. In his poem "The Naming of Cats," Eliot explains why cats need names that sound respectable and _____.

4. Jellicle Cats, he claims, are good-natured and full of _____.

5. He lists the _____ and varied exploits of Macavity the Mystery Cat.

6. He describes two wildly playful cats whose _____ antics can destroy a room.

7. Any cat, Eliot cautions, will resent an _____ on its privacy.

8. To make friends with a cat, he suggests offering a generous _____ of cream or caviar.

9. Most of Eliot's works are serious, but this volume is an _____.

10. Even if you don't _____ like poetry, you will like this amusing book.

Correctly combine the word roots and suffixes shown to form words from the review list.

11. survey + or = _____   16. miracle + ous = _____

12. dismay + ed = _____   17. envy + es = _____

13. rally + ed = _____   18. victory + ous = _____

14. reply + ed = _____   19. convict + ion = _____

15. venom + ous = _____   20. apply + ion = _____

Spelling Power

Proofreading Application

Lessons 17–20

Read the imaginary daytime television listings below. Find and circle the twenty misspelled review words. Then, on the numbered lines, write the correct spelling for each circled word.

1. 7:00 A.M.: *Lonely Highwais*, starring M. T. Rhoades and Dustin Dewinned
2. 7:30 A.M.: *Paiment Is Due,* starring Anita Cash and Zelda Carr
3. 8:00 A.M.: *The Courteus Crooks*, starring May I. Robbia and Woody U. Mind
4. 8:30 A.M.: *Get Plaiful with Math*, starring Adam Upp and Delores Carmen de Nominator
5. 9:00 A.M.: *Summer Lazyness*, starring T. V. Zonn and Hannah Meda Remote
6. 9:30 A.M.: *Luscius Chocolate Recipes*, starring Del Lectable and Olivia Face
7. 10:00 A.M.: *Ambitios Woodworkers*, starring Nick Knacks and Paddy O'Furniture
8. 10:30 A.M.: *The Most Luxurius Cruise Ship*, starring Les Gogh and Ima Witchoo
9. 11:00 A.M.: *Getting Permition*, starring Ken I. Pleeze and Aldo Anything
10. 11:30 A.M.: *Relaiing Secrets*, starring Cody Ryder and Dee Cipher
11. 12:30 P.M.: *Careers in Pharmacys*, starring Philip Prescription and Candy Reed D'Label
12. 1:00 P.M.: *Funnyest Farm Videos*, starring Bill E. Goat and Chick N. Little
13. 1:30 P.M.: *That Makes Me Furios!* starring Madison Wett-Henn and Haven Major-Fitts
14. 2:00 P.M.: *In Denyal*, starring I. M. Knott and Don B. Leevitt
15. 2:30 P.M.: *Kids of 1776—They Joined the Revolucion,* starring Judy Calls and Amos True
16. 3:00 P.M.: *Melt Your Tention Away*, with Ben N. Stretch and Daley X. Ercize
17. 3:30 P.M.: *Suspision of a Crime*, starring Sir Valence and Justin Case
18. 4:00 P.M.: *Easyer Cooking*, with Cole Cutts and Pete Zah
19. 4:30 P.M.: *Buoied by Hope*, starring Ray Zalight and Donna Frett
20. 5:00 P.M.: *The Cowboy Tradicion*, starring Chuck Waggons and Tex Asteers

1. _____
2. _____
3. _____
4. _____
5. _____
6. _____
7. _____
8. _____
9. _____
10. _____
11. _____
12. _____
13. _____
14. _____
15. _____
16. _____
17. _____
18. _____
19. _____
20. _____

Spelling Power

Lesson 21: The Suffixes -ant and -ent

Word Bank

patient	abundant	excellent	observant	descendant
fragrant	resident	brilliant	confident	transparent

Key Concepts

The suffixes -ant and -ent are used with adjectives and nouns.

Nouns: defend**ant**   resid**ent**
Adjectives: reli**ant**   differ**ent**

1. Because these suffixes sound the same, you must memorize spellings of -ant and -ent words. Try to visualize these words as you learn them.

2. Many word roots change form when -ant or -ent is added.

   defy → defiant   excel → excellent

   observe → observant   appear → apparent

3. Some words ending in -ant or -ent have no familiar word root.

   patient   *fragrant*

Spelling Practice

Put each word from the Word Bank in the correct column.

Words ending in -ant

1. _____
2. _____
3. _____
4. _____
5. _____

Words ending in -ent

6. _____
7. _____
8. _____
9. _____
10. _____

Spelling in Context

Write the words from the Word Bank that best complete the sentences.

1. Jeff's grandmother, a gardener and a glassblower, is a _____ of a small town.

2. Her garden is always filled with _____ multicolored flowers.

3. Jeff is _____ that no one crafts better glassware than his grandmother.

4. His grandmother often crafts _____ vases so that no color will distract viewers from the flowers.

5. Jeff is proud to be her _____.

LESSON 21 continued

Proofreading Practice

Read the paragraph below. Find the five misspelled words and circle them. Then, on the numbered lines, write the correct spelling for each circled word.

Around 400 B.C., a group of brilliant sculptors lived in West Africa. These people, the Nok, fashioned human figures of clay, creating excellant likenesses. The patiant and observent sculptors captured details of hairstyles, jewelry, and facial features. The Nok also crafted tools and weapons of iron. Over the centuries, they taught other groups to smelt iron ore, which was abundent in the area.

1. _____   3. _____   5. _____

2. _____   4. _____

Spelling Application

Listed below are six more words that reflect the Key Concepts you have learned.

accident   apparent   consistent   elegant   important   pleasant

Use the words to complete the Tom Swiftie puns below. Circle the -ant or -ent in each word that you write.

1. "That was no _____! You meant to spill your soup on me," said Tom hotly.

2. "You look _____ in your long dress," said Tom formally.

3. "I love the _____ crunch of this cereal," said Tom crisply.

4. "Are you ready for that _____ math exam?" asked Tom testily.

5. "With this new baseball bat, my hitting's strong and _____," said Tom bashfully.

6. "I don't see the jewels; it's _____ that they're locked away somewhere," said Tom safely.

Spelling Power

Lesson 22: Adding Prefixes

Word Bank

predict	discourage	discomfort	unfortunate	export
prehistoric	disadvantage	unfavorable	unexpectedly	exclaim

Key Concepts

1. Prefixes change the meanings of words and word roots.

   dis-: not; the opposite of   *dis + comfort = discomfort*

   ex-: out; away from   *ex + port (carry) = export*

   pre-: before   *pre + dict (say) = predict*

   un-: not   *un + fortunate = unfortunate*

2. Keep all the letters of a word root when you add a prefix.

   dis + similar = dissimilar   *pre + read = preread*

   un + natural = unnatural

Spelling Practice

Choose the words from the Word Bank that are related to the words below. Add the correct prefix to each word. Write your choices on the lines.

1. ? + favorable = _____
2. ? + dict (say) = _____
3. ? + courage = _____
4. ? + port (carry) = _____
5. ? + advantage = _____

6. ? + historic = _____
7. ? + expectedly = _____
8. ? + claim = _____
9. ? + comfort = _____
10. ? + fortunate = _____

Spelling in Context

Write the words from the Word Bank that best complete the sentences.

1. For our carnival act, I'll pretend to _____ the future.

2. I'll emerge quickly and _____ from behind a dark curtain.

3. People will _____ in surprise when I appear.

4. It's _____ that I can't find a crystal ball to use.

5. Don't laugh at my plans—you'll _____ me!

LESSON 22 continued

Proofreading Practice

Read the paragraph below. Find the five misspelled words and circle them. Then, on the numbered lines, write the correct spelling for each circled word.

In preahistoric China, farming began around 6000 B.C. China's first written records date from 1700 B.C., the time of the Shang Dynasty. Many people lived well in that era. Weavers made clothes of silk to reduce the disscomfort of summer heat. Smiths crafted bronze tools for local use and for eksport. Slaves, however, were at a dysadvantage. Their living conditions were harsh and unnfavorable. In 1100 B.C., the slaves rebelled, helping to overthrow the Shang rulers.

1. _____   3. _____   5. _____

2. _____   4. _____

Spelling Application

Listed below are six more words that reflect the Key Concepts you have learned.

discourteous   exchanged   exhale   prearrange   precaution   unheeded

In the right-hand column are word roots. Combine them with the prefixes in the left-hand column to form the words in the list. Use the Key Concepts as guidelines. (Can you form any other words using these prefixes and word roots?)

Prefixes	Word Roots
dis-	arrange
ex-	caution
pre-	changed
un-	courteous
	hale (breathe)
	heeded

1. _____   4. _____

2. _____   5. _____

3. _____   6. _____

Spelling Power

Lesson 23: The Prefix *in-*

Word Bank

import	imprint	insight	inaccurate	immobile
immigrate	inhale	inexpensive	innumerable	impatience

Key Concepts

1. The prefix *in-* often means "in" or "on":
   in + hale (breathe) = inhale

2. The prefix *in-* sometimes means "not":
   in + accurate = inaccurate

3. Change the prefix *in-* to *im-* when a word root starts with *m* or *p*:
   in + mobile (moving) = immobile
   in + port (carry) = import

Spelling Practice

Choose the words from the Word Bank that fit the following definitions. Write your choices on the lines.

_____ 1. to breathe in

_____ 2. not countable; many

_____ 3. not exactly correct

_____ 4. to bring goods into a country

_____ 5. lack of patience

_____ 6. to migrate to a country

_____ 7. not costly

_____ 8. seeing in depth; understanding

_____ 9. not moving

_____ 10. to print a mark on something

Spelling in Context

Write the word from the Word Bank that best completes each sentence.

1. The American Cookie Company plans to _____ cookies from Denmark.

2. They'll _____ the A.C.C. logo on the Danish company's label.

3. They need to check the list of contents to be sure that it's not _____.

LESSON 23 continued

4. Their delivery trucks will stay parked and _____ until everything is in order.

5. I can't wait to _____ the aroma of those delicious cookies.

Proofreading Practice

Read the paragraph below. Find the five misspelled words and circle them. Then, on the numbered lines, write the correct spelling for each circled word.

     Charles Steinmetz (1865-1923) created ways to make electricity practical. This science pioneer overcame inumerable obstacles. Born with a damaged spine, he was treated with inpatience and scorn by other children. He was a genius at math, but he had to quit school. Shackled by poverty, he left his native Germany to inmigrate to America. He soon found imexpensive housing and a laboratory job. There his innsight was appreciated, and he began a brilliant career.

1. _____   3. _____   5. _____

2. _____   4. _____

Spelling Application

Listed below are six more words that reflect the Key Concepts you have learned.

| impartial | impossible | impress | inactive | independent | indigestion |

Use the above words to complete the imaginary book titles.

1. *They Achieved the* _____, by Will I. L. Bee

2. *Causes of* _____, by Maia O. VerEatin and Joe Cookin

3. *Living an* _____ *Life*, by Hugo Yourway and Lyle Gomine

4. *Don't Be* _____—*Stay Fit!* by A. Robics and X. Ercise

5. *How to* _____ *Your Neighbors*, by Moe Dalawn

6. *Where to Find an* _____ *Fan at Playoff Time*, by I. N. Urdreems.

Spelling Power

Lesson 24: Nouns with Unusual Plurals

Word Bank

Singular:	oasis	fungus	radius	cactus	alga
Plural:	oases	fungi	radii	cacti	algae

Key Concepts

Some English nouns are borrowed from Greek or Latin.
These nouns have unusual singular and plural forms.

1. Use the following pattern to form the plural of many singular nouns ending in *-sis*.

Singular:	crisis	thesis
Plural:	crises	theses

2. Use the following patterns for many singular nouns ending in *-us* or *-a*.

	-us	**-a**
Singular:	cactus	antenna
Plural:	cacti	antennae

Spelling Practice

Put the words from the Word Bank in alphabetical order. After each word, write *S* for singular or *P* for plural.

1. _____
2. _____
3. _____
4. _____
5. _____

6. _____
7. _____
8. _____
9. _____
10. _____

Spelling in Context

Write the words from the Word Bank that best complete the following sentences. Be sure to choose the correct singular or plural form.

1. Like other desert plants, a _____ needs very little moisture.

2. Mushrooms, yeast, and molds are all _____.

3. A _____ is one kind of plant that lacks chlorophyll.

4. An _____ is a single-celled green plant.

5. If you measure the _____ of circles, you can calculate the area of the circles.

Name _____ Date _____ Class _____

Proofreading Practice

Read the paragraph below and find five incorrect singular and plural forms. Circle each error. Then, on the numbered lines, write the correct form of each circled word.

We know the Sahara as a scorching desert. Not even cactae grow there. Oasises are few and far between. A Saharan oases may be no more than a shallow pond, murky with algi, offering the only water within a radii of many miles. Yet once the Sahara was green. Between 8500 and 4000 B.C., it was a land of rivers and forests. People there fished from canoes and hunted crocodiles, hippos, giraffes, and elephants.

1. _____   3. _____   5. _____

2. _____   4. _____

Spelling Application

Listed below are eight more words that reflect the Key Concepts you have learned.

Singular: analysis   antenna   larva   octopus
Plural: analyses   antennae   larvae   octopi

Write the word suggested by each science-fiction film title and blurb. Be sure to use the correct singular or plural form.

_____ 1. *Eight Arms, No Legs*—You can't escape this monster's crushing grip!

_____ 2. *Invasion!* Hordes of giant caterpillars from Mars!

_____ 3. *Broken Aerial*—Alone in space, millions of miles from Earth, with her radio transmitter smashed—can she survive?

_____ 4. *The Inchworm That Ate Indianapolis*—Will your city be next?

_____ 5. *The Formula*—A heroic chemist has only one chance to unlock the secret of a deadly Venusian potion!

_____ 6. *Terrors at the Tide Line*—They rise from beneath the sea, grasping sunbathers in their tentacled arms . . .

_____ 7. *Fearsome Feelers*—Attack of the creepy crickets!

_____ 8. *Rogue Suns on the Rampage*—Scientists race to discover why these wild stars defy the laws of physics—and how to stop the stars before they destroy Earth!

Spelling Power

Unit 6 Review
Lessons 21–24

abundant	alga	cactus	descendant	disadvantage
discourage	export	fragrant	immigrate	impatience
imprint	inaccurate	innumerable	oases	patient
predict	radii	radius	resident	unfavorable

Choose the review words that best complete the sentences. Write your choices on the lines.

1. A _____ is a measurement in a circle; it is also a bone in the lower arm.

2. Lee has both arms in casts because he broke both his _____.

3. He rode his skateboard into a thorny rosebush and became a _____ in the hospital.

4. His skin was covered with _____ scratches and punctures.

5. To cheer him up, we brought him a prickly-pear _____ in a flowerpot.

6. The spiny plant has one _____ yellow flower.

7. The plant seldom needs watering, since water is not _____ in the desert.

8. It would be _____ to say that deserts have no water at all.

9. Even the barren Sahara has many _____ with ponds and plants.

10. Pond scum is one example of a(n) _____, a primitive water plant sometimes found in deserts.

Correctly join the word roots and affixes to form the review words defined below. Then use the word list at the top of the page to check your spelling.

11. im + migrate = _____: to move into a country

12. pre + dict = _____: to foretell

13. reside + ent = _____: one living in the area

14. dis + courage = _____: to deprive of hope; to dissuade

15. im + print = _____: to make a mark (v.); a clear mark or pattern (n.)

16. un + favorable = _____: not helpful or promising

17. descend + ant = _____: offspring

18. ex + port = _____: to ship goods out of a country

19. dis + advantage = _____: difficult condition

20. im + patience = _____: low tolerance for delay or annoyance

Spelling Power

Proofreading Application

Lessons 21–24
Read the "terse verse" rhymes below. Find and circle the twenty misspelled review words. Then, on the numbered lines, write the correct spelling for each circled word.

1. prihistoric villain – cave knave
2. brillient Emperor Napoleon – smart Bonaparte
3. inmobile fringe – still frill
4. fungae in the graveyard – mushrooms on the tombs
5. perceptive and charming – imsightful and delightful
6. luggage at a desert pool – suitcases at an oases
7. transparant soda pop – clear root beer
8. watchful butler – observent servant
9. unffortunate little Charles – unlucky Chuckie
10. descomfort in Madrid – pain in Spain
11. get rich selling algi – succeed with seaweed
12. more imexpensive pager – cheaper beeper
13. weep about prickly plants – cry about cactae
14. the kind to bring into the country – the sort to inport
15. excellant ocean – terrific Pacific
16. confidant of a trip through Europe – sure of a tour
17. shout about the e-mail insult – eksclaim about the flame
18. stop breathing – fail to imhale
19. costume worn unnexpectedly – surprise disguise
20. the toadstool that's least old – the fungis that's youngest

1. _____   8. _____   15. _____

2. _____   9. _____   16. _____

3. _____   10. _____   17. _____

4. _____   11. _____   18. _____

5. _____   12. _____   19. _____

6. _____   13. _____   20. _____

7. _____   14. _____

Spelling Power

Lesson 25: Words with Greek and Latin Roots

Word Bank

graph	autograph	photograph	biography	geography
vision	television	telephone	telescope	microphone

Key Concept

Many words in the English language come from Greek and Latin words.

<u>Phonograph</u> comes from the Greek *phone* (sound) and *graphos* (writing).

<u>Television</u> comes from the Greek *tele* (afar) and the Latin *visio* (sight).

Spelling Practice

Write the words from the Word Bank under the correct headings. Two words will be written twice.

1. From *graphos* ("writing")

_____

_____

_____

_____

_____

2. From *tele* ("afar")

_____

_____

_____

3. From *visio* ("sigh")

_____

_____

4. From *phone* ("sound")

_____

_____

Spelling in Context

Choose the word from the Word Bank that best completes each sentence.

1. My uncle's _____ was improved by his recent eye surgery.

2. During the concert, the _____ needed some adjustment.

3. I drew a _____ of population changes for my science project.

4. Our knowledge of _____ can help us read maps.

5. Kim and I watched our favorite _____ program on Sunday night.

LESSON 25 continued

Proofreading Practice

As you read the article below, circle the five misspelled words. Write the correct spelling for each circled word on the lines that follow.

Roma Acropolis will present a review of her new biogruphy, *Galileo,* on July 15 at 2:00 P.M. Following the talk, Ms. Acropolis will sell her books. If you request an autograf, she'll include a photogeraph of herself standing near a model of Galileo's telscope. For more information about this event, telefone 555-0001.

1. _____   3. _____   5. _____

2. _____   4. _____

Spelling Application

Below are four words with Greek or Latin roots. Use the Key Concepts to match each word with its meaning and write the word on the blank. Then write a sentence using the word.

megaphone   paragraph   supervision   telecast

_____ **1.** a group of organized, related sentences

_____

_____

_____ **2.** control and guidance of people or jobs

_____

_____

_____ **3.** a television broadcast

_____

_____

_____ **4.** a handheld device used to amplify a voice

_____

_____

Spelling Power

Lesson 26: Plurals for Nouns Ending in *o*

Word Bank

trios	heroes	piccolos	radios	dominoes
echoes	videos	pianos	tomatoes	kangaroos

Key Concepts

1. Add *s* to form the plurals of nouns that end in a vowel + *o*.

   stud**ios**   kaz**oos**

2. Add *s* to form the plural of most nouns that end in a consonant + *o*.

   phot**os**   banj**os**

3. Add *es* to form the plural of the few nouns ending in a consonant + *o*. (Your dictionary may list more than one possible spelling for some plurals.)

   pota**toes**   mosqui**toes**/mosqui**tos**

Spelling Practice

Choose words from the Word Bank to form the plural of each word below. After you write the correct plurals, draw lines between syllables to show the number of syllables in each word. Use a dictionary with this exercise.

1. echo _____

2. domino _____

3. radio _____

4. kangaroo _____

5. trio _____

6. hero _____

7. piccolo _____

8. tomato _____

9. video _____

10. piano _____

Spelling in Context

Write the word from the Word Bank that best completes each sentence.

1. Please slice the _____ for our luncheon salad.

2. Baby _____ are known as joeys.

LESSON 26 continued

3. Our class produced several _____ in which we interviewed people from the neighborhood.

4. You need basic math skills to play the game of _____.

5. Have you seen the memorial to _____ of World War II?

Proofreading Practice

Read the following article from a student newspaper and circle the five misspelled words. Then write the correct spelling for each circled word on the lines below.

What a great success our spring concert was! In my mind, I still hear echos of the audience's enthusiastic applause. In the first act, two students played a duet on grand pianoes. In the second act, two trioes performed. The first group played a waltz on piccoloes; the second group played a marching song on trumpets. Unfortunately a baseball game was being broadcast at the same time. Several students who had their radioes on were told to leave.

1. _____   3. _____   5. _____

2. _____   4. _____

Spelling Application

Below are nine words that reflect the Key Concepts you have learned. Circle the words in the word maze and write the words on the lines below.

altos   arias   igloos   mangoes

mottos   patios   portfolios   rodeos   tornadoes

```
s  o  i  l  o  f  t  r  o  p
e  a  g  a  s  r  o  a  a  m
o  r  l  u  l  d  o  t  s  o
g  i  o  d  e  t  i  i  o  t
n  a  o  o  s  o  o  r  a  t
a  s  s  a  s  r  a  s  c  o
m  t  o  r  n  a  d  o  e  s
```

1. _____   4. _____   7. _____

2. _____   5. _____   8. _____

3. _____   6. _____   9. _____

Spelling Power

Lesson 27: Plurals for Nouns Ending in *s, sh, ch,* and *x*

Word Bank

addresses	blemishes	porches	mailboxes	radishes
faxes	branches	stomachs	canvases	sandwiches

Key Concepts

1. To form plurals of most nouns ending in *s* or *x,* add *es.*

   clas<u>ses</u>   ta<u>xes</u>

2. To form plurals of most nouns ending in *ch* or *sh,* add *es.*

   coa<u>ches</u>   ra<u>shes</u>

3. Exception: nouns whose final *ch* sounds like \k\.

   monar<u>chs</u>

Spelling Practice

Look at the Word Bank to find the plural form of each word listed below. Write the plural form and the number of the Key Concept that applies to it.

1. blemish   _____

2. canvas   _____

3. fax   _____

4. branch   _____

5. sandwich   _____

6. mailbox   _____

7. stomach   _____

8. porch   _____

9. address   _____

10. radish   _____

Spelling in Context

Write the word from the Word Bank that best completes each sentence.

1. Sometimes the _____ of trees get heavy with fruit.

2. People send _____ so that others can receive important papers quickly.

LESSON 27 continued

3. On summer nights, our neighbors like to sit on their _____.

4. I needed to gather all of my friends' _____ to complete my party invitations.

5. In the country, most _____ have metal flags that are pulled up when outgoing mail is in the box.

Proofreading Practice

Read the paragraph below and circle the five misspelled words. Write the correct spelling for each circled word on the lines that follow.

We invited a group of artists to set up their canvasess in our park. All morning the artists worked on still lifes of a vegetable basket. The carrots and onions were smooth and had no blemishs. The red and white radishs were perfectly formed. During lunch break, we served the artists tuna sandwichs and punch. When their stomaches were full, the artists went back to their easels.

1. _____ 3. _____ 5. _____

2. _____ 4. _____

Spelling Application

Below are eight words with endings that reflect the Key Concepts you have learned. Complete the puzzle with the words from the list.

annexes	choruses	compasses	epochs
eyelashes	skirmishes	stitches	suffixes

Across
1. groups of people who sing together
3. brief conflicts
6. divisions or periods of time
7. buildings used as additions to another building

Down
1. instruments that determine and show directions
2. loops or knots of thread made by a needle
4. word elements added to the end of a word
5. hairs that grow on the edge of the eyelids

Spelling Power

Lesson 28: Plurals for Nouns Ending in *f* and *fe*

Word Bank

chiefs	sheriffs	loaves	lives	ourselves
wives	roofs	calves	cuffs	hooves

Key Concepts

1. To form plurals of most nouns ending in *f,* add *s.*
   belie<u>fs</u>   cli<u>ffs</u>

2. To form plurals of most nouns ending in *lf,* change *f* to *v* and add *es.*
   she<u>lf</u> → she<u>lves</u>   ha<u>lf</u> → ha<u>lves</u>

3. To form plurals of most nouns ending in *fe,* change *f* to *v* and add *s.*
   kni<u>fe</u> → kni<u>ves</u>   li<u>fe</u> → li<u>ves</u>

4. Exceptions include:
   leaf → leaves   gulf → gulfs

Spelling Practice

Match each word in the Word Bank to the Key Concept that applies to it. Then write the word under the number of the appropriate Key Concept.

1	2	3	4
_____	_____	_____	_____
_____	_____	_____	_____
_____			

Spelling in Context

Write the word from the Word Bank that best completes each sentence.

1. The _____ of various Native American tribes sometimes met for peace talks.

2. In old cowboy movies, the _____ rode horses to track down cattle thieves.

3. The outlaws knew they were in trouble when they heard the sound of the horses'
_____.

4. In the movies, the cowboys always tucked their pants _____ into their boots.

5. We _____ bought boots on a recent trip to Wyoming, but we don't plan to track down cattle thieves.

LESSON 28 continued

Proofreading Practice

As you read the paragraph below, circle the five misspelled words. Then write the correct spelling for each circled word.

In the days before modern machinery, the lifes of farm families were very difficult. Both husbands and wifes shared the chores, often working from dawn until nighttime. Women tended to the cooking and baking. Their freshly baked loafes of bread were set out to cool along with pies and cakes. Farm children were expected to help feed chickens, pigs, and calfes. The job of repairing roofes was left to the men.

1. _____ 3. _____ 5. _____

2. _____ 4. _____

Spelling Application

Listed below are the plural forms of five more nouns that end in *f* or *fe*.

beliefs   knives   safes   whiffs   wolves

Write the plural forms next to the singular forms on the lines below.

1. belief _____   4. safe _____

2. knife _____   5. whiff _____

3. wolf _____

Decode the words from the list and write the words on the lines provided. Use the code grid as follows: 15-31-51-15-43 would be ELVES.

	1	2	3	4	5
1	A	B	C	D	E
2	F	G	H	I/J	K
3	L	M	N	O	P
4	Q	R	S	T	U
5	V	W	X	Y	Z

1. 52-34-31-51-15-43 _____   4. 12-15-31-24-15-21-43 _____

2. 52-23-24-21-21-43 _____   5. 43-11-21-15-43 _____

3. 25-33-24-51-15-43 _____

Spelling Power

Unit 7 Review
Lessons 25–28

blemishes	branches	calves	canvases	cuffs
echoes	geography	graph	hooves	kangaroos
lives	microphone	photograph	pianos	roofs
stomachs	telescope	videos	vision	addresses

From the list above, choose the word that best completes each sentence. Write the word in the blank.

1. Giraffes and _____ are my two favorite animals.

2. At the library, I found _____ and books about how these animals live in the wild.

3. One video was produced by a naturalist who had studied the _____ of giraffes for seven years.

4. She took a _____ that shows how a giraffe bends down for food.

5. Like cattle, giraffes digest their food with four _____.

6. Did you know that giraffes' eyes give them extended _____ so that they can see what's behind them?

7. Female giraffes are called cows, and their offspring are called _____.

8. From their _____ to the tops of their heads, adult giraffes measure nearly twenty feet tall.

9. This height helps them reach high _____ of trees so that they can eat leaves and buds.

10. If giraffes lived in towns, imagine what they would do to the _____ of houses!

Choose the word from the list that matches each of the following definitions. Write the word in the blank.

11. mailing information on envelopes _____

12. rolled pant legs have these _____

13. artists often paint on these _____

14. the study of maps and the layout of the earth _____

15. an optical instrument used to study distant objects _____

Use the remaining words from the list to write five sentences of your own.

16. _____

17. _____

18. _____

19. _____

20. _____

Spelling Power

Proofreading Application

Lessons 25–28
As you read the letter below, find and circle the twenty misspelled review words. Then write the correct spelling for each circled word.

Dear Terry,

Grandma and I were pleased to receive your faxs showing the writing award you won. By traditional mail, that would have taken a week! But we do miss the good old days when people could greet the mail carrier in person and people checked their mailboxs every day.

We always had lots to talk about among ourselfs. Even without telvision, we heard news on our radioes. Some of us were lucky enough to have a telephone. To make a call, we put a nickel into a slot and then asked an operator for the number.

My fondest memory is how we sat on our front porchs to watch local parades. First came the sheriffes and chiefes of the police and fire departments. War heros and other veterans followed close behind. Even their wifes took part, carrying flags and banners. Getting a hero's autoguraph was the highlight of my summer! The last group was the high school band who marched in rows as they played drums, piccoloes, and trumpets.

After the parade, everyone gathered for a potluck dinner. Some people brought loafs of bread for sandwichs. Others shared their homegrown tomatos and radishs. Apple cider and pie completed the meal. A few children played dominoz; others formed trioes and entertained us with songs.

Terry, since you're an award-winning author, how about writing my biogeraphy to tell about those good old days?

Love,
Grandpa Louie

1. _____ 8. _____ 15. _____
2. _____ 9. _____ 16. _____
3. _____ 10. _____ 17. _____
4. _____ 11. _____ 18. _____
5. _____ 12. _____ 19. _____
6. _____ 13. _____ 20. _____
7. _____ 14. _____

Spelling Power

Lesson 29: Compound Words

Word Bank

timetable	newsletter	rain check	part-time	outer space
candlesticks	earthquake	full-length	title page	self-portrait

Key Concepts

1. Compounds may be closed, hyphenated, or open.
   baseball   time-out   free throw

2. To spell a closed compound, keep all the letters in both words—even if the result looks odd.
   busybody   freshwater   bookkeeper

3. Hyphenate most compounds that include *self, full, part,* or *great.*
   self-esteem   full-grown   great-grandson

Note: A hyphen is sometimes added to an open compound that is used as an adjective. Use the dictionary to help you spell compound adjectives.
   ice cream (noun)   ice-cream cone (adjective)
but: free throw (noun)   free throw lane (adjective)

Spelling Practice

Put the words from the Word Bank in alphabetical order. Label each compound: C for closed, H for hyphenated, or O for open.

1. _____
2. _____
3. _____
4. _____
5. _____
6. _____
7. _____
8. _____
9. _____
10. _____

Spelling in Context

Write the word from the Word Bank that best completes each sentence.

1. Let's check the train's _____ before we leave for the station.

2. Grandmother's silver _____ are used for special occasions.

LESSON 29 continued

3. When you draw a picture of yourself, you are making a _____.

4. Once the storm began at the ballpark, everybody was given a _____.

5. Our family receives a _____ announcing special events at school.

Proofreading Practice

As you read the paragraph below, circle the five misspelled words. Write the correct spelling for each circled word on the lines.

My sister works parttime at Barton's Bookshop. Last week my grandfather took me there to shop for my birthday present. I checked the titlepage of a book about outer-space to see who the author was. Then I changed my mind and decided to buy a book about Turkey's earth quake. It included several fulllength reports from scientific journals and photos of the damage taken from outerspace.

1. _____ **3.** _____ **5.** _____

2. _____ **4.** _____

Spelling Application

Match each of these compound words to the word or phrase that has the opposite meaning. Write the word on the dotted lines. After you have filled in the blanks, read the boxed letters. The answer tells about something important to all of us.

credit card	full-grown	great-aunt	homecoming	ice pack
nighttime	outfield	self-pity	skyscraper	wildlife

1. newborn ☐ _ _ _ - _ _ _ _ _

2. cash _ ☐ _ _ _ _ _ _ _ _

3. pride _ _ _ _ - _ ☐ _ _

4. leave taking _ _ _ ☐ _ _ _ _ _ _

5. great-uncle _ _ _ _ _ _ - _ _ ☐ _

6. house pets _ _ _ ☐ _ _ _ _

7. log cabin _ _ _ ☐ _ _ _ _ _

8. daytime _ _ _ ☐ _ _ _ _ .

9. infield _ _ _ _ _ ☐ _ _ _ _

10. heating pad _ _ _ ☐ _ _ _ _

Spelling Power

Lesson 30: Words Often Confused

Word Bank

accept	hardy	morning	cymbal	prey
symbol	pray	except	hearty	mourning

Key Concepts

Some words sound alike but have different meanings and spellings. There are several ways to remember the correct spelling of these tricky word pairs.

1. Use memory aids:

   mourning – unhappiness   cymbal – clang!

   morning – before noon   symbol – stands for. . .

2. Use your knowledge of roots and affixes:

   except – to leave out: *ex* (out) + *cept* (take)

   accept – to receive: *ad/ac* (toward) + *cept* (take)

Spelling Practice

Put the words from the Word Bank in alphabetical order. Their meanings are already in the correct order.

1. to receive willingly; to be content with   _____

2. percussion instrument   _____

3. to leave out, *or* other than   _____

4. rugged and tough   _____

5. warm; unrestrained   _____

6. time between sunrise and noon   _____

7. grieving   _____

8. to ask humbly   _____

9. creature that is hunted   _____

10. mark or object standing for something else   _____

Spelling in Context

Write the word from the Word Bank that best completes each sentence. For help, check the definitions in the Spelling Practice above.

1. Inuit elders watch a wolf chase its _____, an ailing caribou.

2. All the caribou _____ this one can easily outrun the wolf.

LESSON 30 continued

3. There is no sorrow or _____ for the caribou, for the Inuit know that the wolf's actions will strengthen the herd.

4. The elders understand and _____ the balance of nature.

5. Animals, like people, must be strong and _____ to survive in the Arctic.

Proofreading Practice

Read the paragraph below. Find and circle the five words whose spelling does not fit their meaning. Then, on the numbered lines, write the correct spelling for each circled word.

Welcome to the New Year's celebration! The time: 580 B.C. The place: ancient Babylon. With the mourning sun's first rays, the festive sounds of drum and symbol announce the holiday. At midday, a grand parade features a dragon, cymbal of the god Marduk. Crowds throng the city. Priests stage a ritual drama to prey for abundance in the coming year. Finally everyone returns home to enjoy a hardy feast.

1. _____   **3.** _____   **5.** _____

2. _____   **4.** _____

Spelling Application

Listed below are four more word pairs to help you practice the Key Concepts you have learned:

coarse	descent	foul	right
course	dissent	fowl	rite

Use the code to match each word with its meaning. Write the words on the lines.

Code:

a	c	d	e	f	g	h	i	l	n	o	r	s	t	u	w
!	@	^	#	$	%	()	&	*	+	?	=	>	<	[]	~

1. ritual or ceremony: = & < #   _____

2. hen or rooster: $? ~ *   _____

3. downard motion: ^ # > @ # + <   _____

4. off limits, in a game: $? [] *   _____

5. rough to the touch: @ ? ! = > #   _____

6. correct; *or* opposite of left: = & % () <   _____

7. disagreement: ^ & > > # + <   _____

8. route; subject plan: @ ? [] = > #   _____

Spelling Power

Lesson 31: Words Often Misspelled

Word Bank

background	rumor	exhaust	parallel	fascinating
necessary	preparation	director	environment	permanent

Key Concepts

1. Commonly misspelled words may include schwa sounds, silent letters, or consonant clusters.

   od_o_r   _p_sy_ch_ology   cup_b_oard

2. Use memory aids to help you spell words correctly.

   _cup_board → "cup" storage

   Fe_br_uary → "br(r)" (for chilly)

   Try inventing memory aids of your own.

Spelling Practice

Write each word from the Word Bank next to its pronunciation.

1. _____ rōō′mər

2. _____ prep′ə rā′shən

3. _____ bak′ground′

4. _____ ig zôst′

5. _____ di rek′tər

6. _____ par′ə lel′

7. _____ nes′ə ser′ē

8. _____ fas′ə nā′ting

9. _____ pur′mə nənt

10. _____ en vī′rən mənt

Spelling in Context

Write the word from the Word Bank that best completes each sentence.

1. On the first day of camp, the _____ welcomed us.

2. She said she likes knowing the _____ of every camper.

3. We were told not to believe every _____ we hear.

4. I'm happy that we sleep in _____ cabins instead of tents.

5. The cabins were built side by side, in _____ lines.

LESSON 31 continued

Proofreading Practice

As you read the paragraph below, find and circle the five misspelled words. Write the correct spelling for each circled word on the lines.

Richard E. Byrd explored the fasinating world of the Arctic and Antarctic. Facing such a brutal envirament took great courage. For each expedition, Byrd and his crew spent many months in preperation. Of course they had to pack up every necassary item they could think of. Hopefully they would not exaust their supplies of food and research instruments.

1. _____   3. _____   5. _____

2. _____   4. _____

Spelling Application

The following words are sometimes misspelled for reasons mentioned in the Key Concepts. Circle schwa (ə) sounds, silent letters, and consonant clusters. Then complete each list of related items with the appropriate word.

adequate	athletics	competent	government
odor	psalm	separate	

1. smell, scent, _____

2. divide, break up, _____

3. qualified, able, _____

4. sports, games, _____

5. administration, ruling system, _____

6. sacred poem, hymn, _____

7. satisfactory, enough, _____

Name _____ Date_____ Class _____

Spelling Power

Lesson 32: Multi-syllable Words

Word Bank

| gymnasium | contained | imagination | variety | updated |
| preferred | auditorium | typical | invitation | curiosity |

Key Concepts

1. You can improve your spelling by understanding syllabication. In most words, each syllable has one vowel sound.
be | lieve   fo | li | age   ex | pla | na | tion
sa | tis | fac | to | ry

2. In some past-tense words, -ed is sounded together with the last syllable.
pro | grammed   con | fessed

3. In other past-tense words, -ed is sounded as a separate syllable.
di | gest | ed   ce | ment | ed

Spelling Practice

Write each word from the Word Bank under the correct heading.

2 Syllables   **3 Syllables**   **4 Syllables**   **5 Syllables**

_____   _____   _____   _____

_____   _____   _____   _____

Spelling in Context

Write the word from the Word Bank that best completes each sentence.

1. Someone who has a vivid _____ often enjoys reading science fiction.

2. Mom made sure that my lunch box _____ a special dessert.

3. I need an _____ version of the computer manual.

4. The _____ of most detectives inspires them to look for clues.

Copyright © by The McGraw-Hill Companies, Inc.

Spelling Power   Grade 6   77

LESSON 32 continued

Proofreading Practice

As you read the invitation below, find and circle the six misspelled words. Then, on the numbered lines, write the correct spelling for each circled word.

The Drama Class of Sloan School presents its third annual varity show. This year's theme is "A Typcal Day in the Life of Sammy Sloan." The show will be held in our school auditorum on February 21 at 7:00 P.M. During intermission, refreshments will be served in the gymnasim. This invition is for everybody in your family!

P.S. If preferrd, you can attend the dress rehearsal at 1:30 P.M..

1. _____ 3. _____ 5. _____

2. _____ 4. _____ 6. _____

Spelling Application

Ten multi-syllable words appear below. Find and circle the words in the maze. Then use the Key Concepts to help you write the words under the correct heading. Draw lines to separate the syllables in each word. Use a dictionary if needed.

approved	communicate	concealed	created	dictionary
edible	international	personality	pollution	society

```
d i c t i o n a r y o u p
e l c o m m u n i c a t e
v e z h i y j o r o r e r
o x k a e t e e k n m o s
r i s v e d a u l c r e o
p o l l u t i o n e t p n
p s i g e s l b i a k u a
a m x d u e l a l l r i l
l a n o i t a n r e t n i
s k i w e b m i t d i f t
c l u p c a s o c i e t y
```

2 Syllables	3 Syllables	4 Syllables	5 Syllables
_____	_____	_____	_____
_____	_____	_____	_____
	_____	_____	

Spelling Power

Unit 8 Review

Lessons 29–32

accept	cymbal	fascinating	hardy	invitation
morning	mourning	necessary	newsletter	outer space
parallel	part-time	permanent	pray	prey
rain check	rumor	timetable	title page	updated

For each quotation below, write the word from the list that best connects to its meaning.

1. The game is rescheduled because of bad weather. _____

2. Don't believe everything you hear. _____

3. RSVP by June fifteenth. _____

4. If we had checked this, we wouldn't have missed the train. _____

5. Read about the food drive at school next month. _____

6. Who's the author and publisher of this book? _____

7. I'll close my eyes and hope for a good grade. _____

8. Sorry, we can't afford to give you a full-time job. _____

9. What lively music our marching band plays! _____

10. This is where I'd like to send my annoying little brother! _____

Match each of the following words with a word from the list above that has an opposite meaning. Write the word from the list in the blank.

11. evening/_____

12. temporary/_____

13. boring/_____

14. rejoicing/_____

15. unessential/_____

16. hunter/_____

17. weak/_____

18. old-fashioned/_____

19. reject/_____

20. perpendicular/_____

Spelling Power

Proofreading Application

Lessons 29–32
As you read the following story, find and circle the twenty misspelled words. Then write the correct spellings for the words on the lines.

Noise in the Attic

It happened last winter vacation when I visited Aunt Bea and Uncle Dan. Their snow-covered grounds made a great enviroment for sledding. Eccept for me, there were no visitors that week.

As I do on a typecal visit, I helped with the dinner preperation. After a heardy meal of beef stew and a variaty of homemade goodies, Uncle Dan and I sat down for a game of chess. Their cat, Theo, was curled up nearby. Since Aunt Bea didn't want me to exaust myself on my first day, she urged me to get some rest. There was blanket on the sofa, but I prefered to sleep upstairs in my cousin's old room.

About midnight a crashing sound jarred me from a deep sleep. My imaganation went wild! Were we in the midst of an earth quake? Were there burglars in the house? After checking the downstairs rooms, I made my way up to the attic.

Almost as big as a gymnasum, the attic containd more items than you could count. I spotted an old baton, a cymbol of my aunt's glorious backround as a band director. Mom used to tell me how grand she looked, dressed in a full length gown, standing on the stage of the school auditorum.

As I stood admiring Uncle Dan's self portrait, I heard a noise behind me. In fear, I grabbed some brass candle sticks to protect myself. A screeching "meow" alerted me that Theo was in the attic. "Oh, no!" I thought. She was probably the one to blame for the terrible noise I had heard earlier. "Theo," I said, "your curiosety almost killed you!"

1. _____   8. _____   15. _____

2. _____   9. _____   16. _____

3. _____   10. _____   17. _____

4. _____   11. _____   18. _____

5. _____   12. _____   19. _____

6. _____   13. _____   20. _____

7. _____   14. _____